W9-DAL-609

SILENT SUN

Sam (Shlamek) Gross

SILENT SUN

Solomon Gross

Cornwall Books
New York • London • Toronto

Cornwall Books
440 Forsgate Drive
Cranbury, NJ 08512

Cornwall Books
25 Sicilian Avenue
London WC1A 2QH, England

Cornwall Books
P.O. Box 39, Clarkson Pstl. Stn.
Mississauga, Ontario,
L5J 3X9 Canada

The paper used in this publication meets the requirements
of the American National Standard for Permanence of Paper
for Printed Library Materials Z39.48-1984.

Library of Congress Cataloging-in-Publication Data

Gross, Solomon.
  Silent sun / Solomon Gross.
    p.   cm.
  ISBN 0-8453-4840-X (alk. paper)
  1. Holocaust, Jewish (1939–1945)—Personal narratives.   2. Gross,
Solomon.   I. Title.
  D804.3.G75   1992
  940.53'18—dc20   91-58258
                                                              CIP

PRINTED IN THE UNITED STATES OF AMERICA

This book is dedicated to my father,
Abraham Gross,
and to all those who pleaded for help,
and no one listened.

Here is a universe as confined as a trap, where the sole heroes are the victims, where muteness is for the intrepid only.
—Cynthia Ozick

I am pusillanimous. I want to speak.
—Solomon Gross

Contents

Acknowledgments

I would like to express my appreciation and gratitude to Sam E. Bloch, Mannes Schwarz, Charles Ross, and Kurt Tusk for their unswerving encouragement and assistance in helping me fulfill my late husband Sam's wish to have his story published.

DORIS GROSS

Prologue

The other day my blond, blue-eyed grandson, Nicholas, announced to his grandma, "I am going to study Hebrew next week." To her question, "Why Hebrew?" he replied, "Grandma Dorka, don't you know I come from the Jews?"

So here we are. For more than half a century, life has been preparing me to write this book. Yet it took only one sentence from my six-year-old grandson to teach me how to begin.

I, too, come from the Jews—the Jews of Poland. Now my most ardent wish is that Nicholas, his delightful little sister Kimberly, and all our children to come will have a less painful time coping with their heritage. I hope the story of my experiences will be of some help.

SILENT SUN

SWEDEN

North Sea

DENMARK

Baltic Sea

U.S.S.R.

Kaiserwald ▪ RIGA
• JUNGFERNEOF

■ NEUENGAMME

STUTTHOF

Malchow
■ RAVENSBRÜCK
Bromberg
Thorn
Bialystok
TREBLINKA

WEST
Unterlüss
Hennigsdorf ■ SACHSENHAUSEN

BERGEN-BELSEN ■
EAST ○ Berlin
Braunschweig Brandenburg
GERMANY Magdeburg
• Gelsenkirchen
GERMANY
Schwarzheide
CHELMNO ▼
• Christianstadt
POLAND
○ Warsaw

LUBLIN

Essen Arolsen
Hessich-Lichtenau Sömmerda Gröditz GROSS ROSEN
Würtegiersdorf
Freiberg
Breslau-Hundsfeld
Waldenburg
Markstädt I
Freiburg
SOBIBOR ▼
MAIDANEK

■ BUCHENWALD

Allendorf
Geisenheim Neustadt
Prague
Zwodau
Ober Altstadt
Ludwigsdorf
Weisswasser
AUSCHWITZ
Monowitz
Bobrek
Günteichen
BELZEC ▼
CRACOW/PLASZOW
BIRKENAU

LUXEMBOURG
Langenbielau

■ FLOSSENBURG
Trautenau
CZECHOSLOVAKIA

Nuremberg

FRANCE
○ Stuttgart
Strasbourg ○
NATZWEILER
Kaufering DACHAU
Landsberg
Gusen ■ MAUTHAUSEN
• Ebensee
Danube R.

AUSTRIA
HUNGARY

SWITZERLAND

See detail map

EUROPE

■ MAIN CONCENTRATION CAMPS
▼ EXTERMINATION CAMPS
• Subcamps

0   60   120 miles

0   100   200 km

Forget

Province of Breslau

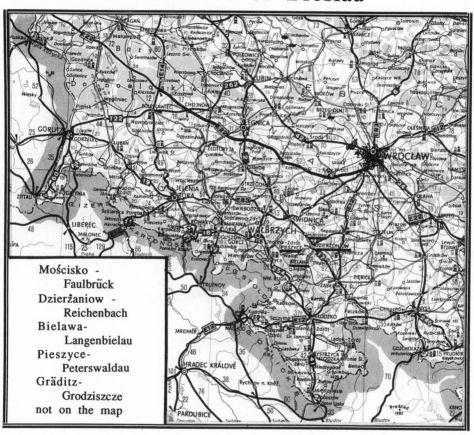

Mościsko -
    Faulbrück
Dzierżaniow -
    Reichenbach
Bielawa-
    Langenbielau
Pieszyce-
    Peterswaldau
Gräditz-
    Grodziszcze
not on the map

1
Reflections: 1939–1940

It was the first week of September 1939. Long caravans of Polish cavalry were passing beneath my windows—endless numbers of empty wagons, their wheels squeaking on the cobblestone road, pulled by sad and tired horses.

By nightfall the squeaking had stopped. "Good!" I thought. "They've passed and are making a stand somewhere." But I was wrong. After a whole day, the manure of thousands of horses carpeted the road so thickly that it silenced the noise. When the pathetic army finally passed, it became hauntingly quiet. The eerie silence lasted until the following evening. Then, in the dark, we heard the hum of muffled engines. Fearfully we peeked through the curtains and saw large open military trucks, each with two rows of helmets lined up ominously along the sides.

"How can they ride so quietly?" I wondered. And then it dawned on me. Of course! The manure—by then half a meter deep—kept the wheels silent, but not for long. As the carpet ripped to shreds, the engines started roaring furiously, and our hearts sank.

In a way, these events foreshadowed what was to come—danger, followed by deceptive calm, followed by greater dangers and disasters far greater than anyone had ever imagined.

Chrzanów, November the 5th A.H. 1940 5 A.M.

More than a year had passed since the war started. And what a year it was. In the beginning we feared mostly the scourge of poison gas, which never materialized. But what came, in quick succession, was much worse: vicious murders and assorted brutalities against the Jews; the unforgivable behavior of our Polish neighbors; the fall of France; the string of German victories

15

culminating in the occupation of most of Europe. Then our hopes were totallly shattered by the incredible and devastating alliance of Mussolini with Hitler.

The fall of 1940 produced a lull, with the Germans apparently digesting their successes. Willingly, even gladly, we accepted the false sense of security. Despite the horrors and disappointments of the past year, we were hungry for life and managed to laugh, and even dance once in awhile to the tune of the then-popular Lamberthwalk. After all, Great Britain, which ruled a quarter of the world, was still free and had never yet lost a war. So what if they had disappointed us bitterly so far? Eventually, we were sure, they would come through.

The glorious month of October was coming to an end and so was the welcome interlude of calm. At the beginning of November, the Germans issued a directive to the Judenrath to deliver 300 volunteers for a special Labor Detail. And thus I found myself standing or, rather, swaying in the wind, at 5 A.M. on that little street named after the poet Adam Mickiewicz. In front of me stood the ever ominous Catholic church, behind me the public school where I spent so many pleasant, even if sometimes difficult, hours. Waiting with trepidation for what might come next, I hoped that at least the sun would break through those masses of threatening clouds and give my freezing bones some warmth and hope.

Standing there, confronting cruel reality for the first time in my life, I realized that I was trapped. Yesterday I was still a relatively free man—in spite of the German forces around me and the cruelties they displayed, I still knew no one would stop me from running. Where? Toward the Russian border, 200 kilometers away. Walking at night, moving like an animal only in darkness, and hiding during the day, I could have made it.

But how does an only child leave his parents behind? Perhaps it was only an illusion of freedom, but certainly, yesterday the cage was a lot larger. "Now I'm really trapped," I thought. I did not realize then that I had by chance chosen one of the very few avenues left that gave a chance of survival. Here I stood, feeling not only cold and fearful, but stupid, as well. "What am I doing here?" I asked myself. "I didn't have to volunteer." But I came nevertheless. Why? Because I was desperately hungry for freedom—any freedom, at any cost. To be 17 and the only child of an overprotective Jewish mother in prewar Poland could easily make uncertainty and danger seem a worthwhile gamble.

When I decided to report voluntarily, my parents naturally panicked and did not want to let me go. They relented only after they were persuaded that it was important to show the German authorities compliance and willingness to work, and that because the Judenrath had more than enough volunteers, all family supporters and only children would surely be sent home. And so I would have been, except that two boys ran away at the last minute and a friend, Berek Grajower, and myself were used as substitutes.

When I started to leave, with a casual "See you tomorrow," my father's face became ashen gray, his eyes revealing enormous pain and a depth of feeling and understanding I had never witnessed before. This was more than a premonition—he must have been sure that this was the last time he would see me. From the beginning this image added to my agonies, fading slowly only after many years. Even today, I still quite often see his face, distorted with pain.

Rumors had it that we would be sent to nearby Silesia to work on important projects in fantastic surroundings, with weekend passes and many other fringe benefits. Nevertheless, my spirits were very low and my body in little better condition as I and the other 299 volunteers, surrounded by soldiers with their bayonets drawn, marched to the train that took us to that "fantastic" forced labor camp *(Zwangsarbeitslager)*, Sakrau.

2

Sakrau—"Basic Training"

The conditions in Sakrau were very tough but not horrible, compared to later concentration camps. We still were allowed some individuality—our own clothes and every once in a while, a package from home. Despite such luxury, those first six months were, for me, by far the most difficult to endure.

Since the war a number of my friends, especially Itzchak Bacon, have repeatedly asked me, "How did you do it?" Knowing my origins well, they were totally puzzled by the fact that I had managed to survive. "You," they asked, "The proverbial soft-boiled egg! How is it possible?"

One reason for writing this book is to answer those questions. Many elements contributed to my survival against all odds. While I hope the lessons I learned will never need to be put to the test by any of my readers, I present them in hopes that they may prove useful in dealing with today's problems.

The phenomenon of luck I can't deny, nor can I explain it. I can only deal with logic. The list of survival factors that comes to my mind includes Optimism, *against* all logic; Youth, with its endless power of resilience; the Arts, yes—music, literature, paintings, especially the heroic and romantic—which gave me hope and inspiration to be optimistic against all logic; a sense of Humor always, no matter how macabre the situation—gallows humor if need be—those who lost the ability to laugh were lost indeed; Enthusiasm, lots of it. But perhaps most important of all was a sense of responsibility and an inner need to Care not only for oneself but for others.

The great Mickiewicz (who by the way also comes from the Jews) expressed it best in his "Ode to Youth" written in 1820 at the age of twenty-two.

Soar high above us all
And with the sun's eye
Penetrate the vastness of mankind
From end to end!
For you the nectar of life
Tastes sweet only
When with others shared

Młodosci! ty nad poziomy
Wylatuj, i okiem słonca
Ludzkosci cale ogromy
Przeniknij z końca do końca.
Młodosci! tobie nektar zywota
Natenczas słodki, gdy z innymi
    dzielę:

Yes, caring kept us going, many mornings when getting up seemed just too painful. How easy it would be just to let go and rest forever. . . . Then would come that nagging reminder in a corner of the brain: You are not alone. It was just enough to provide the missing surge of energy, then suddenly you're up and ready to fight for another day.

Work!

I pity those who use their ingenuity and energy to avoid work. It must be a disease, to hide and listen to your stomach growling from hunger pangs, watching the time clock move slowly, about one second in the span of one minute. How lucky I was to get involved, forcing myself to like whatever I did, no matter how nasty or difficult. No time to look at the clock or think food; we had to work to stay alive, so why not make the best of it? In addition, I gained the added bonus of learning a number of professions.

The Reich's Autobahn

Our first task, once we got to Sakrau, was to build the new autobahn. Our good fortune was that the eight kilometers of road we were assigned to build ran smack through the privately owned field of local Silesian peasants. Most of them were Catholics, fearful of Hitler, ethnically attached to their Polish origins, and all spoke the strange Silesian-Polish dialect. Our first assignment was to save their sods for replanting. Two spades long, one wide, all day long we cut . . . two by one, all week long, the monotonous two by one. The few hours a week I had spent riding a bicycle at home hardly prepared my legs to push a spade into the ground ten hours daily. Our hands were in even worse shape.

In due disrespect, I must pause to describe our supervisors— our German foremen, most of whom probably spent their lives building roads. If this was their vocation, hating Jews must have been their avocation. They competed against one another to see who would turn those delicate, but still subhuman, lazy Jews into efficient road builders faster. They got sadistic pleasure from pushing, cajoling, torturing, and beating us all day. But worst of all was the twenty-minute lunch break. They made sure to face us while devouring their triple deckers filled with lard, a thermos of hot coffee standing by. Most of us had swallowed our ration in the morning before leaving for work, whether out of hunger, fear of it being stolen, or sheer lack of restraint. Our next meal, consisting of a hot potato soup, was a good seven to eight hours away.

I did not believe I would make it through the first day, but the terror of the rod kept me and the rest of us moving. After the first week I felt I had aged to ninety, too tired even to eat. The first to give were our nice, soft leather shoes, cut in half at the arch. As a substitute we were given wooden clogs, with canvas tops, which might have been fun to walk in, but not ten kilometers a day. A whole new set of muscles grew in our calves, hurting like hell. The next problem was snow and nasty winds. Our bodies felt like sieves, the wind penetrating every hidden nerve in our flesh. After that came the frost.

With the onset of winter, the ground froze and we had to give up cutting sod. Frankly, after the terrible monotony of piling up mountains of grass, we were praying for a change. And we got our wish. Overnight we became a snow-clearing brigade. With shovels on our shoulders, in our wooden shoes, we marched endlessly to clear obscure, rarely used country roads, an obvious effort to keep us occupied. After the sod training, it was hard to get used to the weightless snow. But worst of all were the seven hours of walking with no more than about three hours of shoveling.

Once in a while, a thaw would come. You might guess that this would be a blessing, but it was not so. We lived in wooden barracks with open spaces in the walls through which the wind blew strongly enough to knock things off our tables. A cast iron stove stood in the middle of our room, which housed twenty. The coal ration, in the form of rectangular synthetic bricks the size of cinder blocks, lasted at most four hours. We burned it as quickly as the stove could absorb it. The stove pipe would get red hot up to the ceiling and we felt heavenly until about midnight. But thereafter we shivered under our horse blankets, yet we were too tired for the cold to keep us awake. The worst problem was that our socks, soaked from the blessed thaw, dried only on the side exposed to the hot pipe, while the other side remained wet and cold. A smack of a whip hurts terribly on impact, but to put on wet frozen socks before 5 A.M. in a freezing, pitch dark room is a lasting, excruciating torture. The misery lasted long after we began walking, which did not happen for at least two hours after we got up. Thanks for the thaw; I will take the frost.

"Wo habt ihr die Kohle?" ("Where Did You Hide the Coal?")

Eventually we rebelled against this ordeal and turned to stealing coal whenever and wherever we could. Unfortunately we exercised no restraint and depleted the camp supplies very visibly. This prompted our civilian camp administrator *Lagerführer* to search the barracks. (His name was Shaya; our Jewish town council, the Judenrath, showered him with gifts on his frequent visits, hoping to alleviate our plight.) He charged in, screaming, *"Wo habt ihr die Kohle?"* but all the coal was already in the stove, except in room number 18. The unfortunate boys in room number 18 had stored a few bricks under a bunk for the next cold night. As a punishment they had to stack their bricks neatly on top of a blanket, and then carry them, walking barefoot, forming a funeral procession. They had to march slowly around the campgrounds for the rest of the night singing Volga-Volga and other assorted funeral marches. Despite the frozen feet and sleepless night, we all had a good laugh and kept stealing coal, but more discriminately.

By January 1941, our legs had toughened up and we became used to the wooden clogs. Our bodies still drew on the juices left from home and we kept up our daily marches.

For a while fears about our libido spread through the camp. Rumors circulated that we were being fed chemicals that would inflict a slow but permanent impotence. But as long as it was not a question of outright castration, these fears eventually were relegated to the back of our minds. Soon we realized that the problem was poor nourishment and extreme fatigue.

Our carefully coded postcards from home kept us informed of the military transports that moved day and night toward the Russian border. Hope kept us going. With hope in our hearts we kept the back roads of Silesia clear of snow.

One very cold morning, in those initial months of what I call my basic training, our still decent Jewish administrator, *Judenältester* S. Selinger (in later years *Judenältester* became sinister masters of life and death) picked me out of the lineup and told me that I would remain inside the camp to take care of his office plus other chores around the premises. With every bone in my body frozen and aching, I suddenly felt the sun smiling at me. My friends would not have been human if they did not feel envy. Minutes later, I found myself in a warm clean office, with a slice of buttered bread and a hot cup of coffee just for me. "Unbelievable," I thought, "how close paradise can be to hell. Oh! Yes, here we go! Paradise—Hell—did I have to read Faustus? Damn stupid fantasy!"

Many years later, I found myself in a movie house watching *King Rat*. In a hunger-starved Japanese POW camp, the handsome British prisoner is being treated to scrambled eggs and sausage by George Segal, the "King." After he finishes licking his fingers in a stupor of delight, he asks the King, "Now, when do I lick thy ass?" Such were my feelings when I took that first sip of hot coffee. On top of it, I was keenly aware that my friends were already about five kilometers on the road. How could I enjoy my newfound heavenly comfort? My foolish, perhaps childish pride kept me from accepting this morally questionable opportunity to ease my lot. With no little fear in my heart I thanked Mr. Selinger gracefully, but asked to be sent back to shoveling snow the next day. My reward was immediate. The reception I received the next morning, marching with my fellow sufferers was overwhelming. I was bursting with pride, as everyone treated me very respectfully and all were exceedingly helpful. I thus learned my first important lesson . . . stay clear of certain kinds of favors!

A big thaw came; the splendid sun showed its face in full glory. We were clearing a runway at a god-forsaken, obscure airfield in the middle of nowhere. A clear, blue sky and a hot sun easily outdid our efforts and before long, we were standing knee-deep in mud and water. We were fifty men, with two uniformed guards and one civilian supervisor. Suddenly something snapped in every one of us. Our shovels, propelled by some hidden command, swung watery snow in every direction. Our guards sensed something going wrong, but did nothing; the foreman, confused, could not demand that we shovel snow because there was none left. I was getting very frightened. A dangerous sense of freedom filled the air, too overpowering to resist. Another minute and all would have been lost—after all, where could we run? With three Germans dead, the whole camp would have been immediately machine gunned. Somehow, miraculously, reason prevailed. Frozen, wet above our knees, full of apprehension, we sadly started the march back home.

This incident, plus a few other small insubordinations, prompted the Germans to show their teeth. A few days later our infamous nemesis, S.S. Major Lindner, arrived with a new blue-uniformed police commandant. He introduced himself with a long, threatening harangue, closing with the following statement: "Those of you who will not behave properly and produce efficiently will be sent to a concentration camp called Auschwitz. Auschwitz is a place where people come in through a gate and leave through a chimney. The following ten who were reported misbehaving will be the first to be sent there." The ten unfortunate scapegoats were immediately taken away—no one ever saw them alive again. It was also the last time anyone dared to show any open signs of defiance.

Barring unexpected emergencies like heavy snow or railroad car unloading, Sundays were free—relatively free, that is. We spent most of the day cleaning, washing, and mending what was left of our garments. We also did some cooking. The talents of our culinary experts was unbelievable; while it took a lot of ingenuity to make meals out of make-believe ingredients, even more imagination was required to make us believe the results tasted good. On the other hand, food for thought we had plenty of. Aside from our chores, we spent most of our time politicking. News was picked up from newspapers discarded by the guards and from the Germans working next to us on the autobahn. Of necessity, we became great experts in reading between the printed lines. Otherwise, listening to the Germans and judging by the headlines only, we would have collectively committed suicide.

The guards and the German personnel employed in our camp were bored stiff. We learned how to stay out of their way, giving them few opportunities to have fun beating us up. To liven things up, they asked our *Judenältester* to organize a *"Bunten Abend,"* an evening of entertainment. While most of us would have preferred to stay in our rooms and rest some more before facing Monday morning, those who possessed various talents jumped at the opportunity to show off their abilities, and sometimes even managed to get an extra ration of food.

In retrospect, I realize that despite our distaste for it, these entertainments benefited our psyche. Among us was a fellow by the name of Kurt Nebel, the son of a well-known Jewish butcher in the border town of Katowice. About twenty years old, he was handsome, big, six feet plus—a towering figure next to us weaklings. He was strong as a bull; where it took four of us to move a heavy chopped-down tree, Kurt did it by himself with ease. Supposedly he drank lots of warm cattle blood right after slaughter. The Germans were impressed. One of our first S.A. yellow shirt guards, who also happened to be among the most brutal, had worked for Mr. Nebel senior a few years previously. He liked Kurt a lot, supplied him with extra food rations and supposedly was for a while in touch with his parents. This did not stop him from treating the rest of us in the most beastly way.

As I have mentioned before, all our tormentors at that time knew the Silesian slang well. Kurt had an exceptional talent for telling jokes in the dialect and was always called on to perform. Most of us had a hard time warming up to his brand of humor, but the guards and the other Germans, watching and listening from the back rows, were rolling with laughter and wouldn't let him go. One story, which he told over and over again, I repeat primarily to demonstrate what made the master race roar with laughter.

Two construction men were standing on a scaffolding, Hans on the second floor, Otto on the first, talking to each other. A third worker, William, appears above them and calls down to Hans, "Hey, be quiet! I got something to tell ya. I just heard that Otto's mother died suddenly. Listen, Hans, you must give him the bad news, but please do it quietly and delicately." Hans scratches his head for a while, then bends over and yells, "Hey, Otto! did you have a mother?" "What da ya mean? Sure I have." "Well, Otto, not any more, now you got shit!" They made him repeat this story to every visiting big shot who came to inspect our camp. Who knows? It might have softened them a bit.

Poor Kurt. The bigger they are, the harder they fall. As the S.A. lost favor and were replaced by the blue uniform police, Kurt lost his support and deteriorated very rapidly. His pathetic decline within a few weeks made it abundantly clear that physical strength alone was not enough to make it.

3

Sakrau—Spring 1941

With the snow gone, the ground soft again, and no more sods left to cut, we were ready to resume building the autobahn. Grading was our next heavy task—filling in a valley here, removing a hill there—work made to order for the students of Yeshivas, sons of tailors and storekeepers, most of whom studied or helped their parents and had never held a pick or shovel in their hands before! Now we laid railroad tracks for the locomotives, loaded and unloaded lorries, assembled giant steam shovels using only a small jack and crowbar. All was based on the principle of leverage and that steel on steel slides easily. Truly remarkable! It brings to mind a Greek saying, "Give me a lever long enough and I will raise the globe."

Credit is due to the German foremen; they were remarkable craftsmen, especially one called Manius, unloading and assembling heavy machinery with the help of ten hungry, inexperienced Jewish boys. Despite the enormous physical exertion, I found it exhilarating to be one of the movers. We were a special battalion: the responsibility and dangers were much greater, but we were accorded a bit more respect. This was a short but interesting interlude; once the machinery was in place, most of the movers had to return to their mundane tasks, though a few wound up helping to keep the locomotives and steam shovel furnaces going.

I met one of them, Levi Kohane, in 1968, in Israel, in uniform. When I asked him what he was doing during the Six Day War, he smiled and answered, "Ride a locomotive to the Suez Canal." Well, we learned something.

Life could have been a lot more bearable in those days had it not been that most German foremen excelled as well or more in the hatred of Jews than in professional skills and ingenuity. Let me disillusion everyone who believes in the innocent bystander: they all delighted in poking fun at our clumsiness, much of which was caused by a lack of preparation and hunger. Swinging the stick and whip was their amusement, not their duty. For example, they would pick six scapegoats, boys of widely varying height, and order them to carry long railroad tracks. When the taller ones buckled upon the weight, the foremen had great fun going to work with their sticks on the tall boys' legs. "Straighten out! Faster, faster, you lazy dogs!" they would yell. This surely had little to do with increasing production. Some of those foremen were sons of the German proletariat whose fathers perished themselves in Hitler's concentration camps.

One morning, an electrician arrived, picked six boys, and asked us to follow him. His belt was loaded with an array of cutters, pliers, screwdrivers, and other small tools. On his shoulder was a pair of iron claws used to climb telephone poles. Each of us was given a spade and a pick with an extra short handle. So equipped, we walked about a quarter of a mile to the side of the future autobahn. I was pleased to notice that we were getting a lot closer to the homes of the peasants and away from the road we had built. Arriving at our workplace, we found stake-outs already in place about a hundred feet apart, in the shape of graves, approximately seven feet long and three feet wide. We were told to dig six feet deep, keeping the holes as narrow as possible. They would eventually accommodate electrical and telephone poles for a maintenance station to be built there. These stations were needed to repair and replace equipment used in building the autobahn.

Delighted to get away from the dullness of grading and loading the lorries, we applied ourselves to our new assignment with enthusiasm. Digging deep, grave-like, narrow holes was no picnic, but as long as we did not encounter hard rock or it did not rain, the task was bearable.

I recall vividly one particular morning, when everything was going wrong. It was raining—one of those spring rains, fine and constant—and the ground was full of rocks. Slowly but surely the rain soaked through every thread of our garments. A downpour would have been welcome, because then we would have had to stop working, but a drizzle was bad. The supervisors, who had proper hoods and overalls, made fun of us. "What's the matter? Afraid of a little rain? You *Schweinehunde*" (You swine dogs). To depress us even further, the beaming Germans gave us the news that Tobruck had just fallen. Africa, the Balkans, all of Europe, victory upon victory—when and how will anyone ever stop him, we wondered.

We had plenty of bad days, but this was one of the worst. Wet, resigned, we stood submerged above our chests in that grave, in water up to our knees. Suddenly a figure in black, almost an apparition, appeared in front of one of the huts. A white container hanging from her arm, she motioned me to come over, all the while looking in all directions. While no one was in sight, I jumped out of my "grave" and slid toward her like a reptile, scared stiff of being spotted. And there she was, a sweet old lady making the sign of the cross and addressing me in Silesian.

"Jesus, Maria, what are they doing to you?" she said. "Here. Take the coffee and bread; it will warm you. Be careful. Leave the can by the ditch and I will get it after dark."

Forty-eight years have passed and I still fight tears when I think of her. We were lucky to work close to those peasant homes. This was the first of many contacts and it was the beginning of a few-months-long romance between a young Jewish boy and the lovely spinster sisters, Tereska, eighty, and Magda, eighty-five. They often took food from their table, risking serious consequences, in order to alleviate our suffering.

Nothing will ever match that first meeting; nothing will ever restore my trust in mankind more than this apparition in black, standing on those steps, holding her white can filled with the sweet nectar of life on that miserable, rainy day in March 1941.

"The Anvil"

Despite our anger and hate toward our oppressors, despite the nagging fear of tomorrow and the enormous hardships, I can't deny the sense of satisfaction upon completing an assignment. We dug those holes, put up the masts, stretched and attached the energy-bearing cables, and awaited the final test. With one move of the lever, the light went on, and the old-fashioned leather belts started moving. We felt a thrill despite ourselves. Even our supervisor could not suppress an ever-so-faint smile. Those Jewish prison *(Häftlinge)* boys had done it after all!

Our supervisor understood every word of Polish although he never admitted it. He, for one, never raised his hand to hit any one of us despite quite a few little mistakes. I knew I would miss this job very much, especially being able to run up and down those poles with the iron claws attached to my shoes. I felt so free up there. I was one of the birds. What pain I felt to have to come down!

With all the machinery in place, hands were needed to run them. By then, I had gained a reputation for being adaptable and eager to work. Everyone started to call me by the nickname *Techniker*. The name stuck and I was always in demand. First cleaning, then operating the drill pressers, lathe sharpeners, and grinders gave me a new insight into the strange world of metals: their behavioral patterns, characteristics, and possibilities. I learned arch and acetylene welding, and much more.

For a while, I worked next to a Polish welder who had volunteered to work in Germany and accepted the status of a *Volksdeutscher,* sort of a "higher-quality" Pole. It may be hard to believe but, despite our plight, strong feelings of jealousy arose when one of us Jewish prisoners excelled in any kind of a job. Of the many dirty tricks used against us, one was particularly nasty.

I made the mistake of letting this welder see that I had a steady hand. While welding together two sheets of aluminum, I produced a perfect seam, which was not easy to do with aluminum. But from the look in his eyes, I realized that I'd better watch out. A few days passed. Then one morning I assisted him in cutting railroad tracks with his acetylene torch. When I moved away to bring over the next track to be cut, he turned the flame on a wrench lying on the ground. When I returned, he called, "Hey, Techniker! Pass me the wrench, the one on the floor." Of all the dirty tricks! Fortunately, he had made it hot enough that I could feel the heat before I grabbed it full force. I escaped with a lot of pain but no serious injuries. I knew then that it was time to move on.

The Germans had just finished installing a set-up for a blacksmith shop. A hand, or rather a foot, was needed to push the pedal of the blower that supplied oxygen to intensify the temperature of the open flame. This became part of my next job. The balance of my time was spent pounding the red hot iron to the rhythm of the mastersmith's little hammer. The sledge hammer I used weighed about 12 pounds, so that after a day's work pushing the foot pedal and wielding the hammer, I had absolutely no trouble falling asleep. Getting up was the big problem. For weeks, I had to use one hand at a time to pry open the other cramped, clenched fist. My biceps and leg muscles hardened and grew, and despite the hardship and pain, I liked my new work a lot. And the compensations that followed were even greater.

During the war, nothing made of metal was available to the civilian population. I learned quickly how to produce utensils that the neighboring farmers were starved for. With the tacit approval of my blacksmith master, I started producing, mostly during lunchtime, a variety of small shovels, hoes, and fireplace stirrers. Nicely shaped with twisted handles, they were truly wrought iron specialties. The closest farmer's fence practically touched our work station—one swing over the picket fence put me into his domain. The farmers paid me with what we needed most: food. I earned enough so that my buddies and I were not hungry.

Eggs were a most desirable luxury. Total production was reserved for the army. To keep my master blacksmith happy and keep his eyes turned in the other direction, I kept him well supplied with eggs (imagine the Jewish prisoner supplying luxuries). Let me confess that I was not in want of eggs myself. Nature was my ally; I never met a chicken that laid an egg silently. Upon hearing the clue, I would be there, ready with a thin nail in my hand to punch a tiny hole in each end through which the still-warm contents of the egg could slip down my throat. Ignorance can be bliss—at that time I knew nothing of cholesterol!

I enjoyed my lessons in forging hot iron and steel. Once, we spent a day and a half producing one axe out of a three-inch-thick rectangular piece of steel with nothing but a couple of arbors to punch the hole for the wooden handle. With only two hammers, we shaped it to perfection, hardened and sharpened it on a sand stone turned by hand. The blacksmith must have gotten a whole cow for it. His usual angry, fire-spitting eyes smiled for once. The toughest job of all was welding two threaded rods to produce an extra long screw. The blacksmith did not trust welding so we had to melt the two prespliced ends and hammer them together with enormous speed before the molten iron would cool. After each welding job, I was ready to collapse.

During this period, I befriended Marek, a fellow inmate about twice my age who was an accomplished tinsmith, respected for his skills by all, including the Germans. Well-read and intelligent, he

had great sympathy for Russia's ideology. An incident I referred
to in an article written forty-six years later will best describe our
encounter.

1987—Two Former Inmates Meet After 46 Years

Early one afternoon in 1987 while strolling in front of the
Jerusalem Museum waiting for it to open, I noticed a small
group of French-speaking people sitting on a bench. Something
about a gray-haired man in the group made me stop, then
walk by again and again—something remotely and hauntingly
familiar. A face from a distant past . . . the eyes, the head . . .
especially the shape of the head . . . but no, it couldn't be! That
man from the past had had fierce red hair . . . and yet, 1941 was
forty-six years ago! Hair turns gray but skulls retain their shapes.
On the other hand, this man speaks French. Absurd! Yet I
couldn't leave without asking.
  "Excuse me, sir: Do you by any chance speak Polish?"
  "Yes, I do," came the reply.
  "Are you perhaps from Klobuck?"
  "Yes, I am. And who are you?"
  "Before I answer, would you mind showing me your hands?"
  At this question, the man's face paled. He slowly lifted his hands
and yes, the little finger on his right hand was missing. Embracing
joyfully, both men together uttered one word: "Sakrau!"
  Their story reached back to early 1941. Sam (Shlamek) Gross, a
native of Chrzanów, Poland, had been detained at age 17 in the
Zwangsarbeitslager (forced labor camp) Sakrau in Germany. He was
assigned to a repair station, serving on the autobahn construction
as a blacksmith's assistant. Marek Swierczewski was a talented
tinsmith whose work was much appreciated by the Germans. A
friendship soon developed between the frightened, inexperienced youth and the more mature, but equally distressed
tinsmith. The older taught the younger many tricks of the trade,
and they helped each other to cope with their tough situation. The
two shared a bunk, Shlamek "upstairs" and Marek "downstairs,"
and would often talk late into the night, sharing thoughts and
fears and sustaining each other with moral support.
  Both men worried about their families. Shlamek's thoughts

were with his parents, who had relied on their only son to scrounge food and other necessities. How would they manage without him? Marek had a wife and a child at home and was deeply concerned for them. As time passed, both men's fears for their families grew.

At that time in the labor camps, if someone was injured or became seriously ill, there was a chance that he would be allowed to go home for a recuperation period. One day, when he was at an extremely low point, Shlamek confided in Marek that he was planning to cut off his finger in hopes that he would be sent home.

"You are young . . . you will survive in one piece," Marek scolded him. "Why ruin your two healthy hands? Germany can't hold on much longer." Thinking it over, Shlamek heeded the older man's wise counsel.

A few days later, however, upon entering the shop, Shlamek was shocked to see Marek being carried out on a stretcher. Shock turned to horror when he learned that Marek, in a desperate attempt to be sent home, had cut off his own finger. He had received word from home that his child was dying, and his wife needed him desperately. But his sacrifice turned out to be futile; both eventually perished.

After the war, Marek Swierczewski found his way to France and rebuilt his life there. Sam Gross eventually settled in the United States, but he never forgot his friend. Through the years, Sam suffered from haunting memories of Marek, who had deliberately mutilated himself because of Sam's idea.

Adapting to Camp Life

Among the many things I learned from Marek, the most helpful was how to manufacture a handy metal container in which to carry liquids without spilling on the road to work. All through my remaining camp years, this container *(menashka)* was my major source of income. Eventually I could produce it from any metal available: brass, galvanized tin, stainless steel. Best of all, however, was aluminum—no welding seams, simply folded over with a tight-fitting cover, flat on the side next to the body, half round on the outside. I describe it in detail because it played a very important part in our struggle for survival. In fact, in 1988, I was standing at a relative's gravesite when someone tapped me on the shoulder. As I turned around, a man who looked vaguely familiar asked me, "You are Shlamek? Are you still making *menashkes?*" As I collected my thoughts, he went on, "Often, they saved me from starvation." Then he added, "And they were made very well too."

Another example: in the winter of 1944, when the real concentration camp had caught up with me and I was freezing in the formal blue-gray striped uniform, with a 1½-inch-wide shaved stripe running down the middle of my head, no longer having any contacts to alleviate hunger, a thought flashed through my mind. I took a chance and made one of those *menashkes* for the all-powerful *Judenältester,* Boruch Meister. I carved his initials and shaped a crown in brass, polished it, and attached it to the front of the little container. It made a hit—he was elated and the next day, I found myself delivering a specially cooked dish to a neighboring all-female camp, where the reigning Jewish (female *Judenälteste*) queen was his ladyfriend. There was an extra bonus for me! Dorka, my future wife, happened to be residing at that time in the same establishment, an authentic, old castle.

However, we are still in Sakrau. After a few more abortive attempts to get home, with my strength depleted, I finally accepted my lot and tried to do my best under the existing circumstances.

One day, I received a signal from a close-by neighborhood farm to come over immediately. The farmer's daughter, who was always very nice to me, was wringing her hands and pleading. "Techniker," she bawled, "My little baby goat broke a leg and must be put away. I can't do it. Would you . . . could you?" Well, that was an assignment I was not prepared for, but I remembered that one of our boys was the son of a ritual slaughterer *(Shochet).* At first, he protested that he had no experience, but the thought of a piece of goat meat was too tempting. With that part of the deed completed, we faced the big problem of how to get a goat through the camp without getting caught. The slightest bulge in our clothes would provoke an immediate, thorough search. And throwing a parcel of this weight over the fence with two guards marching on each side of our column was much too risky. We had to find another way.

The solution came to me late at night, when our stove was ice cold. I got down from my bunk and to the surprise of all, preceeded to break off the hinges holding the cast-iron door. The next morning, I reported the damage and asked for permission to take the stove with me in order to weld the broken hinges back together in our repair station. The policeman in charge could not find anything wrong with that.

"You can do that?" he asked. "Sure," I said, "I work in the welding department." "Good," he nodded. "If I like the job you do, you can fix our half-broken stoves in the station."

The rest was simple. The cut-up little goat covered with wood shavings fit easily into the empty stove. We suspended it on a long stick running through the door opening and the pipe connection, and two men easily carried it back to the camp. It happened to be Chanukah, and what a feast we had! My extra bonus earned me one more nickname. For months to come, everyone in camp called me "the goat."

Our daily lives were studded with such little adventures accompanied always by big scares and risks of getting caught. For example, we often ran out of coal necessary to cook our extraordinary meals. The coal storage cellar was smack across the street from our *Lagerführer* Shaya's windows. One night, when it was my turn to get coal, I somehow slipped on the first cellar step and slid down about fifteen more, hitting on the way each step with the two empty pails I was carrying until I reached the bottom. The racket was absolutely unbelievable! I lay still and breathless, expecting the worst. Twenty skeletons dancing on a tin roof could not have made more noise. Lying down there I saw myself becoming a skeleton soon. A long while passed but nothing happened, absolute quiet . . . a miracle! We discovered the explanation the next day. Shaya, our *Lagerführer*, had a new, young girlfriend. The evening before, they had emptied a few bottles of schnapps and this was what probably saved my life. I made a resolution then and there to take no more trivial chances. I would get the bacon; somebody else would have to worry about the cooking.

Resolutions made are rarely kept, however. As the little storage box under my bunk became depleted, I always found new incentives to take more risks, and I ventured into ever new forbidden territories.

"I will take care of my enemies myself, but dear God! please protect me from my friends!" This saying brings to mind an episode that took place as a result of one of my desperate attempts to get home. I was spending about ten days in the infirmary. One of my buddies, who knew of and benefited from my friendship with the two kind old ladies, Tereska and Magda, slipped into their house one morning while I was still playing sick. To their worried inquiries about my whereabouts, he simply, without batting an eyelash, replied, "Oh, the Techniker . . . he died." The poor ladies were shocked beyond words. With tears in their eyes, they gave him everything they had prepared for me, and more. When I finally made my way once again to their house, they at first turned pale, thinking that it was my ghost who had come to visit. Then they cried and laughed hysterically, forgetting completely about the ugly and inexcusable behavior of my buddy.

In the meantime, the autobahn project was progressing, and soon one could see the outline of the road. We slowly became accustomed to our role as road builders. Thanks to the proximity of the village, some additional food always found its way to us. We were hungry, yes, but not unbearably so. If only we had been permitted to work without chicanery and abuse!

As a rule of thumb, we were rented out to private roadbuilding companies. The firm that worked on our eight-kilometer stretch of the autobahn was Kallenbach GMBH Berlin, headed by an eighty-year-old German blue-blood whose name I don't recall. Once in a while, he paid us visits in his black Mercedes, always exquisitely groomed and impeccably dressed. He rarely left the car; his limousine would pull up close to us, and with his ebony cane, he would jab the driver on the shoulder to roll down the window. All the German foremen hated him. They held their noses surreptitiously because they could not stand the smell of his perfume, which he must have used lavishly. They called him "Old Harbol." "Here he is again with his stink," they would complain. "One can choke from it; it's worse than gas." We loved the hatred they displayed for one of their own, and had fun watching them sticking out their tongues after him.

Below "Von-Harbol," the reigning monarch was chief engineer Ruppert. This devil used to appear suddenly in his four-wheel-drive sports car from nowhere. Instantly, he was everywhere, bellowing and shouting the worst imaginable anti-semitic curses. He kicked the bent-over inmates who were rearranging the railroad tracks, somehow managing to hit their rear-ends all at the same time with his shiny boots. *"Schnell, Schnell,"* he screamed, enjoying himself. "You filthy Jewish sows!" His frequent wild intrusions were, however, baby stuff compared to those of his second-in-command, Engineer Marks. Fatter and more arrogant, Marks was the son of one of the old supervisors under whom we had worked without any serious problems. Junior felt the need to show his superior knowledge and efficiency. He found flaws with whatever we did, picked a few suppposed culprits, and beat and kicked them until they were half dead. He never stopped before his own strength waned. We named him Max the Terror and tried to stay out of his way, to no avail. He always managed to find a couple of victims to satisfy his sadistic lust. We in the repair shop were lucky, since specialists were out of his jurisdiction.

One beautiful, sunny day, I was startled by a comparatively light kick in the behind while wielding my sledge hammer at the anvil. I turned around and faced the mustache and green felt hunting hat of Mr. Ruppert himself.

"Itzik! You come with me!" I dropped the hammer and followed him. We climbed up the embankment, which was loosely filled with sand, and walked toward a vehicle that looked like a tank. It moved on ropes, with a steering wheel sticking out of its side. To guide the ropes, it had a left and right lever.

"Itzik!" he said. "Start it up!" I looked bewildered. His riding boot was coming in my direction. "You dumbbell! You Jewish idiot! Eh! You all know how to count money!" Boom! A kick in the rear. He called over one of the drivers and ordered him to show me how to ignite the monster.

The steering wheel was the starter; by turning it vigorously in one direction, you activated the single cylinder, which had a 10- to 12-gallon capacity. By opening the throttle just right, with luck, one could get the monster puffing. Noon time under the hot sun, it was fairly easy. But in the morning, one had to use a wood alcohol lamp to warm up the nose of the cylinder before attempting to start it. One had to be extremely careful with the wheel. If you were lucky and the machine started, the spikes of the wheel immediately began to rotate with great speed. You had to remove your hand very quickly in order not to get caught. This happened to one of the wise guy *Kapos,* and he walked around for six weeks in a cast. But I am running ahead of myself.

Here I stood in front of that monstrous antique, which was puffing and rattling, like something out of a fairytale. "Get up and drive!" Ruppert barked. "Get up and drive . . . I've wasted enough time!" In utter terror, I mounted the beast, stepped on the gas, and promptly choked it off. It was my good fortune that his boot could not reach me up there. He glared at me, grim with anger, and said, "Next time you do that, you will get a bullet up your asshole!" Then he turned around and vanished.

It will be hard to believe, but for the next couple of months, I drove this monster daily, to everyone's envy and my own great chagrin. What started out as fun turned into a nightmare. Enduring about 120 shakes a minute, for ten hours a day, unprotected from the sun, I rolled the sand back and forth. Sometimes they attached a large trailer in which I hauled sand from a nearby pit. With a few boys on top of the open trailer, I drove through the village unprotected. Because I knew most of the farmers, they handed us food along the way, and we were the envy of the whole camp. Unfortunately, I could not hold any food down because of the constant vibrations. The only thing I managed to swallow was water, which I drank from the pail I carried to refill the radiator.

That constant shaking for ten hours a day took its toll. I became emaciated and sank rapidly. Furthermore, the political situation depressed us severely. These events took place in June 1941. The invasion of Russia started; for two weeks, we were extremely tense, holding our breath as we waited for news. Can anyone imagine our terrible disappointment when, after a total news blackout, we started reading the discarded newspaper headlines and saw the smiles on the faces of our enemies. By then, most of the skilled men working on our project, especially the drivers and heavy equipment operators, had been called up for service. The building of the autobahn was left to the elderly Germans and us. Some of the younger half-wits who were left behind resented that Jewish prisoners could take their places. To prove our inefficiency, they resorted to dirty tricks.

One day I went routinely to pick up my load of sand. When I got back into the sandy surface of our workplace, my fully loaded tractor would not budge. It stood there like a stubborn mule. The chief of the station arrived and immediately noticed that someone had exchanged my air-filled tires for solid rubber ones. It was impossible to move a heavy load on a sandy road on solid rubber wheels. For the first time I heard the chief use some juicy invectives of the sort usually reserved for us on his own kind: *"Die verfluchten Sauhunde!"*

He happened to be a decent fellow. A couple of days later, I appeared in front of him and asked him point blank, "Do you prefer me dead or could you use me for some worthwhile work?" He looked at me, smiled, and said, "Tomorrow, you're coming back to help the blacksmith. Anyhow, he asked for you."

Epilogue: They assigned to my tractor a young German driver known as *Halbwilder,* the Half-Wild One. They also gave him a helper. A couple of days later, the two of them were bringing in a load of sand. While coming down the hill toward the railroad crossing, they belatedly noticed an oncoming train. Not being sure they could make it in time, the *Halbwilder* stepped on the brakes, but the hill was too steep and the load too heavy. He panicked and switched into reverse. The truck stopped. The next day, they brought it in for repair. I am sure that no one has ever seen a ten-gallon cylinder piston and gearbox broken into so many pieces. This was the end of the puffing monster.

How to keep one's cool in a similar situation was demonstrated by one too old for active duty. The autobahn at this point had the steepest allowable grade; the old machinist, probably in his early seventies, had to push about ten empty lorries up to the highest point to be reloaded. He was returning solo, downhill, with the locomotive only, to pick up another lot of empties. Midway on his trip, he had to stop for nature's call. As he got ready to return to his locomotive, he saw to his dismay the ten empties he had left at the top of the hill starting to roll down by themselves. Someone had not secured the wheels properly. As they rolled down, they quickly gained momentum. We all froze, waiting in terror for the collision with the locomotive. But the old man did not panic; he jumped in and started the locomotive rolling downhill, running away from the oncoming load. Methodically, he brought the two speeds into even tempo and thus, when the empty lorries hit the locomotive, the force of the impact was minor. Everyone applauded and we were very happy for him—and more so, for whoever had failed to secure the empty lorries. *His* life wouldn't have been worth a penny!

Once in a while, on far too rare occasions, we came across a gentleman. The surveying Breslau engineer Fuchs was one. He had two helpers who carried his equipment, one of whom was my friend Berek. Recently, I asked him, "Fuchs treated you well? I remember he used to give you bread." "No," said Berek, "he gave us cake." A lovely, kind man—I hope he comes across these lines.

4

The POW Experience

One day in the fall of 1941, I was told to prepare a box of tools and welding equipment to take along for a trip to another camp. We were supposed to repair some broken stoves and windows. After a couple of hours' drive, we arrived in a huge POW complex. Upon arrival, we unloaded a batch of assorted tires we had brought along. In front of the parking lot stood a tent housing a blacksmith workshop. While our guard was busy filling out forms, I approached the blacksmith behind the anvil and tried to explain to him that this is exactly what I do at our camp. Little did I suspect what was in store for me. The man looked at me strangely, pulled out a few cigarettes, handed them to me, and uttered a greeting that was unmistakably "Shalom."

As it turned out, I had landed in the midst of a POW camp consisting of soldiers belonging to the British-Palestine brigade. I was beside myself with excitement, but I am sorry to say that my excitement was not shared so enthusiastically by my fellow Jews. They considered themselves British soldiers and were not anxious to be identified with their Polish brethren. Poor communications were probably part of the difficulty, since they spoke English of which I knew none and my Hebrew was very limited. In any event, it was a great letdown. Imagine! Meeting real-life Jewish soldiers in Germany in 1941 and all I got was a few Egyptian cigarettes.

Our next stop was the Russian part of the camp and there, things were quite different. At this point, I could wish for a pen of a literary genius. The conflict with Russia was in about the fourth month. The environment in which I grew up left much to criticize in terms of general behavior. Except for the great, well-known Jewish talents and personalities, we youngsters could not find much in our midst to emulate. That is how I felt until this visit. That Russian prisoners-of-war-camp was my first direct confrontation with the abyss of humanity. Those soldiers of the Red Army had only been captured two or three months ago; how could anyone sink so low so fast? I'm well aware of the deprivations they experienced, but consider: their food rations were no smaller than ours, the quality of their living quarters no worse, their work no harder, and our mutual oppressors hated no one more than the Jews. There had to be other reasons; as it turned out, I found them soon enough.

Now my reaction was pride. Pride in our own self-control while facing adversities. No matter how meager our rations, they were divided calmly and evenly. We managed to remain human; not so the Russians. A pail of food would be delivered to their room; immediately, twenty prisoners would throw themselves wildly at it, fighting one another until everything spilled and they would wind up licking it off the floor. Their windows were smashed; their stoves, broken; their *Kapos,* always ready to murder. I watched one tall, emaciated Russian buckle under the weight of a sack of cement. The well-fed *Kapo* swung his long black cowboy whip at his calves, and blood shot up like a fountain. Instead of straightening up the poor wretch collapsed like an accordion and fell smack into the wet mud.

I learned later that the Russian soldiers were always watched over by Ukrainians and vice versa. Germans knew how to take advantage of the intense ethnic animosities existing in that army. This was the animal kingdom at its lowest, including even cases of cannibalism. I realize that the Germans were anxious to decimate the Russian army. What surprised me was to see how the poor ignorants played straight into their hands. I watched with dismay how much help the Russian prisoners themselves gave the Germans in accomplishing their task.

There was little I could do to change such devastation. The Russian mechanic assigned to work with me, while telling me all those sordid stories, did not show much of a desire to try to improve his comrades' living conditions. I made his day by sharing with him the few Egyptian cigarettes I got from the Palestine brigade. I was devastated and felt sick, witnessing this ugly, horrible sense of resignation.

How Goodly Are Thy Tents, O Jacob!

Upon my return, I summoned all my friends and reported my experiences. Thereafter, I heard very few complaints.

My own impressions were reinforced recently by the following words of Abba Kovner, quoted by Lucy S. Davidowicz in her epic, *The War Against the Jews 1933–1945:*

Jewish Behavior in Crisis and Extremity

The will to live of Jews in the ghettos contrasted dramatically with the passivity and total resignation that characterized the Russian prisoners of war. Even ghetto Jews who encountered them at forced labor and who often risked their lives to give them bread were appalled at the transformation of human beings into wraiths of wretchedness.

This has been an eventful day. Evening was approaching as we started on our way back. Before leaving the complex, we stopped at what turned out to be the central food depot for all surrounding camps. We picked up a mountain of what must have been horse meat, strings of German frankfurters, and an assortment of other sausages. The driver and guard were in the front seat; I, all by myself on top of an open truck loaded with a cornucopia of the best. Too bad that there is a limit to what one can eat at one time; that evening, I probably beat all records. But it was frustrating the hell out of me not to be able to bring some back to the gang. It got pitch dark; it was very late. Figuring that there was small chance that they would bother to search a single prisoner, I proceeded to wrap myself with frankfurters, from waist to neck. I always dragged my trench coat with me, no matter how warm it was; it had come in handy many times. And so with my secret hidden under my shirt and overcoat, I passed the front entrance gate without problems. The guards let me drag my tools off the truck, and unloaded the meat by themselves. No one afforded me a second look. About 11 P.M., I walked into my room. Like a magician, I started pulling out the booty from under my shirt and coat, to everyone's surprise and delight.

After I told them my story, my companions got busy heating up the franks. While they cooked, I fell asleep—I must have fallen asleep before I hit the mattress. After all, it had been a long day filled with strange emotions. When they woke me to share in the feast, everyone noticed a big swelling on my left cheek. Irony of ironies, this particular evening, as you can well imagine, I was not hungry. But there is always room for a bite of a hot frankfurter. When I tried to take that bite I almost fainted from the pain. My tooth, a rotten molar, aggravated by the wind on top of the open truck, made its presence known, and I got little if any sleep that night. Very slowly, morning arrived. My friends pulled the dentist, Heniek Werner, out of bed early. He took one look and all he said was, "Out." In Poland, most dental mechanics practiced dentistry. They did not need liability insurance, and they were much cheaper than full-fledged dentists. So much for the experience of my surgeon-to-be!

They put me in his chair. The big, buxom nurse, Hane Seminauer, grabbed my head; two guys each, one leg; two more, my arms. And with only an icing spray for anesthesia, the dentist proceeded with the extraction. He grabbed the molar hard, and on the first yank, the decayed tooth broke. I'll make it short. Seven times, he reached into my mouth and finally succeeded in removing the cracked tooth in four small parts.

I knew then firsthand how those characters in Hollywood movies, having bullets removed by amateurs, would feel in reality. If I did not die from pain in that chair, I came very close to it later, choking on the blood clots that kept accumulating all night in my mouth. All of the next day, I was really sick. The following morning, however, I was back swinging my sledgehammer, one side of my face fatter than the other. Oh, youth! with its power of resiliency.

Despite their victories and a most convincing show of normality, the Germans eventually had to abandon the building of the autobahn. And with that, my days at Sakrau came to an end.

Two Breads

Before we left Sakrau we took leave, wherever possible, of the peasants we knew. There was a lot of apprehension and sadness on both sides. The two old ladies, Tereska and Magda, cried and worried about what was in store for us. On the last day, I got hold of two lovely loaves of bread. We were well aware that wherever we were going, some extra food would come in handy. Taking a chance was a necessity. I approached the gate with fear and found my apprehensions to be correct—all inmates had to submit to a search. The Germans wanted to ascertain that no small tools or other valuables were finding their way into our pockets. I was stuck with my two breads, too late to eat or throw away. I had no choice but to move ahead. Sheer temerity saved my skin. I placed the two loaves along the insides of my arms and kept them there with my half-closed hands. Approaching the inspecting guard, I raised my arms to a fully horizontal position, my ever-present trenchcoat thrown casually over my shoulders, my chest pushed out to the limit. I looked the guard straight in his eyes. He could never suspect anyone who was hiding something to have so much audacity. He looked at me and nodded his head. Pass! UH! The trench coat had come in handy again. The two breads proved to be worth their weight in gold in the following few days.

5

Gräditz and Faulbrück

We left Sakrau behind and boarded a train for our next destination. Examining a map today, I see that it could not have been more than 100 kilometers away, though deeper into Germany. The closest known large city was Breslau. After hours of slow back-and-forth train travel, we arrived in a small village called Gräditz. Four kilometers from Gräditz was another little village called Faulbrück. The next two-and-a-half miserable years we spent in those two places. They moved us back and forth three or four times. In retrospect, I am convinced that those moves were initiated by our immediately civilian superiors and their S.S. buddies strictly in order to satisfy their own comforts and needs, while demonstrating their efficiency in supplying Jewish slave labor.

The Vansee Conference, where the official seal of approval for the "final solution" was given, did not take place until the beginning of 1942, although the steps leading to it began years before. In the meantime, we toiled and expended our last drops of energy, hoping to last long enough to get out before our bodies became too weak to be useful. Sakrau, for me, was the most difficult physical experience. That soft-boiled egg had to toughen its shell, or else. . . . With the help of the extra food that I managed to "organize," plus the natural enthusiasm that prompted me to chance any opportunity, however risky, I was able to overcome the initial shock.

Gräditz proved to be a trial of a totally different nature. When we arrived, forty people from other camps were already there. Our group numbered sixty. The problem was that for the next three weeks the hundred lived on rations meant for forty. Due to error or neglect, additional supplies of food did not come until three weeks after our arrival. The food was clean and well prepared, but instead of a dinner dish, we got our meal in a coffee cup. This was hunger at its worst. One more week and out of the one hundred there would have been fifty left, at best.

The normal rations designated for us were 600–700 calories per day. This was calculated to keep us productive for one to two years at most. In my estimation, about 20 percent of that was syphoned off by the *Kapos,* cooks, and other members of our own administration. What was left for the multitude could not keep them alive for long. Unless one found means to augment one's ration, he or she could not survive more than six months. Now, cut those rations in less than half and you will realize how desperate our situation was in the first weeks in Gräditz.

We would march four kilometers to Faulbrück to build a *Bestandslager,* a huge storage complex for military supplies. Everything you can imagine was there except food and ammunition—utensils, blankets, sheets—all, unfortunately, inedible. At dusk, when it was time to start the march back, our energies were totally sapped. We dragged home. My legs started to swell. It felt like the beginning of the end. Within a month one hundred more prisoners arrived and with them, the first load of additional potatoes. The group unloading had to be watched very carefully to be sure they did not devour them raw. Mornings and nights, we started getting potato soups mixed with sandy spinach. The majority of the inmates experienced swelling from water retention. Nevertheless, the soup helped alleviate the hunger pains and gave one an illusion of fullness around the pit of the stomach.

With the second one hundred inmates, the Germans sent us along a *Judenältester.* His name was Stopkovski. The least likely looking fellow one would expect the Germans to pick for leadership, he was short, unassuming, but well-versed in military lingo. Hearing him without seeing him, he could pass for a top-notch professional Wehrmacht drill sergeant. They loved that. In addition, he possessed exceptional organizational talents. Most likely, he would have been very helpful during our ensuing Gräditz calamities, but unfortunately, he overestimated the confidence the Germans afforded him, and made, somewhere, a wrong move. After returning from work one night, we were told that two uniformed S.S. men appeared and took him away. No one ever heard or saw him since.

Sorry, my friend, for us you were the Good Angel that brought us back to life. This is how it happened: on the first day, Berek and I were standing in line to get our evening bowl of soup. Inside the kitchen, in front of the kettle, Stopkovski stood punching out holes in the dinner tickets. When our turn came, we heard the click but found no hole in the ticket. Still very naive, despite our Sakrau experiences, we ran back to him to call his attention to the mistake he had made. He gave us a devilish smile and say, "Ninnies! I don't make such mistakes. Go and get yourself another portion." This was the turning point in our life in Gräditz.

We tried to reciprocate. Berek had an affinity for calligraphy and drawing. I found out the name of Stopkovski's sweetheart; Berek drew the name on a sheet of brass, the letters pierced by an arrow. I cut it out, engraved the highlights, soft-soldered a safety pin on the back using a candle light for heat, and rubbed it with a soft stone to achieve a satin finish. The end result was a very original, nice-looking pin. Stopkovski was delighted. He probably felt like the guy who bet on the right horse. He showed the pin to everybody, including our German cook. This cook was a tiny creature—under five feet—one of his legs considerably shorter than the other, the cook's hat almost taller than he was. Never without his leather whip, always angry, he beat the girls in the kitchen at the slightest provocation. He also must have had a harem, because no matter how many pins I made for him he always came up with another name. This, of course, changed our food situation. It was also my first attempt at manufacturing jewelry . . . but more about that later.

The Koch (Cook)

Around that time we began to venture into the potato storage room next to the kitchen. Knickerbockers were in fashion at the time, and were a blessing with their closed bottoms that served as deep pockets. All our precious cargoes were carried in these pockets. One evening the *Koch* decided, for some reason, to return. Were it not for his limp and special shoes he would have caught us all in the act. Alerted by the noise, we flew to the nearby staircase and ran up as fast as our legs could carry us. The fabric of my trousers must have reached the limit of its strength; one leg ripped open, spilling all the potatoes on the *Koch*. I can still see vividly how, one by one, they hit and flattened his tall white hat.

Hysterical, screaming wildly, he tried desperately to catch up with us, but fortunately it was an uneven contest. By the time he reached our floor, we were under the blankets snoring. He was too embarrassed to start an investigation and search. Cursing viciously, he left. The next day he put an extra heavy padlock on the door.

The building we were thrown into in Gräditz used to be a flour mill, four stories high. The floors were made of wooden boards laid loosely, with spaces big enough for us to converse and pass small objects from floor to floor. A massive staircase led all the way up to the roof, where a large abandoned water tank stood. At first we occupied the ground floor, sleeping on sparsely filled straw sacks.

While being moved senselessly back and forth between Gräditz and Faulbrück, we kept absorbing more and more inmates. By the fall of 1943 we had about 1,700 people, 1,600 men and about forty women. The women worked only in the offices and the kitchen.

Let me give you a bird's-eye view of the camp's layout. Coming off the road through the front gate, one found oneself in a center court of about 120 square feet. On the immediate right, facing the road, stood a low, one-story building, housing the kitchen and a small but richly endowed warehouse, meant for the administration only. Behind it, facing the square, stood the four-story mill. To the left, extending about ¾ of the way across the yard, stood a low barn with about twelve cows and lots of manure. On the left side of the court—vis á vis the mill—was a three-story building housing the police station, with a five-car garage on the ground floor. The first floor was occupied by the *Lagerführer,* his second in command, and their families. On the second floor lived Herr Zuhr and his two daughters, always busy milking cows, shoveling manure, or pushing wheelbarrows. Herr Zuhr was the proprietor of the mill and now was engaged in the cattle business, supplying the Wehrmacht, which eventually sent him to prison for black marketeering. The opening between the barn and three-story building led to the outhouse on the left, the inmate kitchen and its storage rooms on the right. Further out was a barbed-wire–enclosed field, the *Appellplatz* in German, about 300 square feet in size. This was the gathering place for the morning roll calls before leaving for work and for the countdown before dismissal in the evening. This field also served for selection of the damned—fortunately, not too often. And occasionally it became the stage for a display of the gruesome talents of German cruelty.

All of these details play a part in my story.

Fraulbrück, Late Fall of the Year 1941

And so a few hundred of us kept marching the four kilometers to Faulbrück daily. We were building that large warehouse that was supposed to supply the Wehrmacht with all their daily needs, except food and ammunition. The plan called for transforming an abandoned brick factory into an efficient supply house. We loved the layout—a labyrinth full of wonderful hiding places where one could rest and even doze off for a while. Let me point out that what saved us all along was the fact that six men, no matter how efficient, can never watch every step made by a hundred. It is most difficult in an open field; it is totally impossible in an enclosure divided by corridors and walls.

Work was bearable under those circumstances. Our great dilemma was the lack of contacts to get some extra food. We were convinced that a loading railroad platform must exist close by a projected warehouse. We found it eventually, hidden behind overgrown bushes and trees. All of a sudden, everyone was volunteering to clean the weeds and dirt. Our supervisors and guards, oblivious to our needs, were totally surprised.

Until this time, we had never seen or known of the existence of sugar beets, which were used primarily to feed cattle and pigs. Shaped like turnips, they were dirty gray on the outside, creamy white on the inside. We took a bite and discovered they were sugar sweet. Some beets fell off the overloaded wagons and we feasted for awhile on what seemed to be a heaven-sent sweet bonanza. Soon enough, however, we learned that they were not all that pure a blessing. Many of us swelled up awfully; with others, the digestive system rebelled violently. We thought that eating them raw might be causing the trouble, so we set about finding a way to take them. Here my blacksmith experience came in handy.

Among the old buildings, I found a room housing a completely equipped blacksmith shop with an ample supply of the special coal (coke) used for blacksmithing. Feeling that fortune had smiled on me again, I pointed out to the supervisor in charge how many of the windows and doors could not be opened because of broken hinges. Then I showed him the supply of flat stock on hand, made to order for those purposes. He looked at me skeptically, but gave me two boys and let me proceed. Before I ventured to bake the first sugar beet, I produced a perfect set of hinges and attached them to one of the doors, ready for the next day's inspection. I was in business!

One drawback was that various guards and supervisors liked to watch me work. They would stand there watching, while my friends could not wait for them to vanish, eager to put the next beet into the fire. The smell gave us away once in awhile, but most of our tormentors only looked and remarked indignantly, "This is swine fodder. No human would eat that!" Obviously they did not know much about hunger. For a change, I was the cook while others provided the bacon. On the pretext of repairing caved-in stovepipes, they kept damaging the pipes and bringing them in loaded with beets, or turnips, to my fireplace. Eventually, though, we learned that sugar beets, baked or raw, do not make the healthiest of foods. We had to look for other sources.

As we became better acquainted with the new territory, we discovered a narrow creek behind the complex, flowing into a fairly large pond. While active, the brick factory operators had drawn their water supply from it. At this point we first encountered Mr. Eye—yes, that's what we called him. Watch, came the warning, The Eye is coming. I forget his real name; it's possible I never knew it. A giant of a man, he moved about on two crutches, because he had only one leg and one eye. But what an eye it was! There was a disturbing vision in that one piercing eye.

He was the previous owner of the brick factory and a veteran of World War I. We listened with apprehension to the even rhythm of his approaching crutch, not knowing whether to fear him or welcome him. He did not speak much; he just looked and listened, choosing to be a bystander without exercising authority. If he would have informed on us, he could have done a lot of harm, for he, more than anyone else, saw through all our tricks. Despite our better judgment, prompted by fierce hunger, we took a chance and challenged him.

Watching us work, he could not hide his contentment at seeing the improvements we were accomplishing in his old factory, but he never gave us anything. Every morning, we would see him carrying, a wet sack filled with small fish attached to his crutch. Using the pretext of needing to start our fire early, three of us got permission to leave the column immediately after arrival. From an attic, we watched The Eye making his way to the creek and emptying a specially constructed wire trap that caught the little fish on their way to the pond. That was all we needed to know. The next morning, we made certain to be there before him—and the day after, and the day after that. We never took more than a third of the catch. A week or more passed. Then one morning we heard his crutches approaching again. They sounded a little louder, we thought. He appeared, looking more somber than usual; he stood there and just looked. Then raising his crutch and pointing it at me he said, "*Pass mal auf* (Watch it! Watch it!)," turned around and with an increased vigor, left. We never went near that creek again.

A month or so later, I was fixing up an office for Mr. Wind, who was in charge of the whole operation, in the house where The Eye lived. His door was ajar and I could not resist the temptation to glance in. There, on top of the piano, stood two photographs of two handsome, blond, teutonic knights in Wehrmacht uniforms, aged about 20 and 22. Both frames were wrapped in black . . . I had found, at last, the painful secret hidden in his eye.

Der Wind

The monster we called "Der Wind" must have been epileptic. Although I never witnessed a seizure, I saw him many times, beating numerous inmates mercilessly, unable to stop till foam gushed out of his mouth. In his 20s, he was totally disorganized, totally crazy, and it was clear why he was not in the army. He drove everyone nuts, including all the German foremen. Our biggest efforts were devoted to evading him.

One Monday morning he showed up without the keys to his closet. I was summoned to help. As I came in, he was pacing the room like a tiger, foam beginning to appear in the corners of his mouth. It was hard to keep cool. As I looked at the closet door with its hanging padlock, I recalled a similar situation once before when someone tied a knot at the end of a towel and hit the padlock with it. There was not much to lose, as he was becoming increasingly wild. I got a towel, tied a knot at the end, and dipped the knot in water for added weight. I swung it like a baseball bat and pop, the lock sprang open. The "Wind" looked at me, bewildered, confused about how to react, his eyes wild. Then, as the door opened, he noticed a loaf of bread he had left behind last Friday. The loaf was shaped like a large brick; he grabbed it and threw it at me full force. It was hard, like a rock, with green mold growing at one end. It hit me like a brick. Still, we all had a wonderful toasted fiesta. More important yet, I had managed to get a loaf of bread from The Wind—an accomplishment equal to a miracle!

My next experience with this creature was even more unusual. As the construction progressed, someone noticed unused coated copper cables stretched from pole to pole all over the complex. During the war, copper in Germany was a rare commodity indeed. The word "copper" made any task an instant priority. A *Kapo* probably mentioned that I was an expert climber of telephone poles, and I was immediately given a pair of iron claws, a set of pliers, and heavy clippers.

I spent the next few days climbing poles, cutting off and rolling into coils the retrieved cables. My poor helper, Mr. Unger from Zawiercie, and I tried to stretch that job as long as possible. Registered as an electrician, he was an elderly man at the end of his rope, but during this task he started gaining back some strength and was petrified at the thought of going back to his previous drudgery. He tried to slow me down endlessly. I wish I could have accommodated him a bit longer, but there were only so many poles to take care of.

Reluctantly we approached the remaining two, the last of which stood at the very edge of the pond. We had an extremely warm indian summer in the fall of 1941, and this was one of its hottest days. I climbed the very last pole first. By then I had regained my full agility and did not bother to close my safety belt. I cut the first three cables without incident, but when I squeezed my cutter on the last one, the tension remaining between the last two poles let go and I was thrown full force straight into the pond below. I flew like a rock released from a sling. When I hit the water, the heavy iron claws attached to my shoes pulled me straight to the bottom of the lake, which was luckily no more than about fifteen feet deep. I tore loose from the mud and swam quite easily to the surface. At the edge of the pond, a group of boys were grading the surface, preparing it for another structure. The Wind, as usual, was working over one of the inmates. As he heard the splash he turned around, ran over to the edge and with his hands on his hips, stood itching to get at the inmate who had the nerve to take a bath, as he thought, on account of the hot weather. Without waiting until I had climbed all the way out so he could see my irons, he screamed, *"Ferfluchter Schweinhund!* You are taking a bath, wait! I will give you one."* As I climbed further out he saw the claws and recognized me, then stopped like an animal deprived of his bite and said, "Oh, I thought you were taking a swim." He must have felt terrible—for the second time, I had deprived him of the opportunity to lay his hand on me. Too bad!

Approaching Darkness

Akdamuth—A prayer chanted during the Shavuot holiday in praise of *creation*

If all the skies were made of parchment,
If all the waters would change into ink,
If all the reeds would turn into pens,
And all people would become scribes.

It would not suffice to describe in our case the horrors perpetrated by the Germans against the Jews.

Each time I listened to the chant of that mystic poem called *Akdamuth* I thought it most suitable to express the magnitude of those crimes. But then I came across the words uttered by Rudolf Hess, the commandant of Auschwitz, after listening to the prosecutor's statement that it would not be possible to read all the charges because they would fill twenty-one volumes, three hundred pages each, describing his crimes. Therefore the prosecutor said he would open this trial with a simple statement. "You are charged with the murder of four million human beings.—Do you plead guilty?"—"Yes, your honor. Though according to my calculation, I only murdered two and a half million."

The days grew shorter and cooler. The news from home,

brought sporadically by new arrivals, was nothing that could cheer us. The newcomers, who had physically led relatively comfortable lives at home, lived in constant fear of roundups and tried to make the best of every moment, "carpe diem," knowing it could be their last. The euphoria caused by Rudolph Hess's flight to London soon died down completely, leaving everyone deeply disappointed. Russia, to our knowledge, was practically defeated. As the progress toward our own destruction gained momentum, it was small wonder that our spirits were extremely low. Nevertheless, at this point, I personally felt rewarded for having volunteered in the very beginning because the physical exertion of each day's efforts led to a refreshing sleep at night, no matter how dirty, uncomfortable, and cold our quarters were. And we were blessed on that count—our nights were calm.

A little spark of life came after the liquidation of the camps used for the autobahn, when a few more girls arrived. Some of them came from our home town of Chrzanów and knew us well. They all worked in the kitchen and tried to be as helpful as possible, although there was not much they could do. One morning, Rutka Grubner had kitchen duty. Meaning well, she dipped her scoop deeper into the kettle, hoping to catch an extra piece of meat resting on the bottom. This was our lucky day, we thought. In one of our containers (menashkes), we landed a substantial piece of horsemeat. Three of us, Berek, Romek, and myself, shared our food, eating part of it in the morning, and taking the balance along to Faulbrück for lunch. That day we happened to be working out of doors and hid our treasure behind a wall in the shade. But all three of us forgot that the sun does not stand still—at midday, when the time came to devour our feast, we found the cover lifted halfway by explosive fermentation from the hot sun beating on it for some hours. The smell alone could kill. To give you an inkling of what hunger can do, we were not about to give up our meal and proceeded to eat the whole thing, spoon by spoon. (This story is for the benefit of the medical profession.) Three types of digestive systems yielded three different results— Romek turned into a spewing fountain; I couldn't get off the can; but Berek suffered nothing. He looked at us as if he could not understand what the whole fuss was about.

With winter approaching, Gräditz had no facilities available to house 500 or 600 inmates. Because the warehouse was way behind schedule, it was decided to move us to Faulbrück, abandoning Gräditz for the present. We endured the winter of 1941 in terrible conditions in Faulbrück, with no heat or water, and strewn all over the complex. The only consolation was no marching to work. Without the eight-kilometer daily walk, the warehouse building progressed much faster and was completed in the spring of 1942. By then, with the Russian campaign dragging on and priorities changing, some of us were needed in ammuniton factories closer to Gräditz. So, we went back to the old mill in the spring of 1942 to Gräditz, part of us resuming the march to Faulbrück while others walked in the opposite direction to build houses or work in ammo factories. I still worked most of the time in the blacksmith shop. Because the warehouse constantly needed maintenance, I had the chance to resume producing those all-important containers, charging one ration of bread per *menashka,* a price that everyone was very happy to pay. Thus my close friends, helpers, and I maintained bearable living conditions.

Those camps were microcosms of society, with their own laws and means of existence. On a lower level, they were still guided by the principles governing a free community. Left to ourselves, with no interference from our bestial captors, we could have made our lives, despite the extremely meager means, exemplary. The law of supply and demand ruled supreme. Everything had its price: a bread ration, a butter ration, soup, or soap—some would rather wash than eat. A few had even managed to bring along a piece of gold or silver, hidden in their clothes. Finding a buyer or seller was no problem, with everyone living so closely together. As I have mentioned before, a handful of guards, no matter how efficient, cannot fully control every move of hundreds. We worked next to French prisoners of war, who gladly exchanged bread for cigarettes; Greeks, Czechs, and even the German professionals who worked next to us, all were eager to purchase a piece of gold, silver spoon, a cigarette case, for penny-priced food articles. Risks were taken by all involved; too bad that the consequences were borne predominantly by our hides. For us, however, those were the only means available to get a reprieve of our day of execution.

I have stated there were no innocent bystanders; however, once in a while, incidents such as the following took place.

My future brother-in-law, Bernard, worked as a carpenter in a

village called Schweidnitz, located in the opposite direction from
Faulbrück. Twenty-six men were picked up by truck every morning and taken off to build wooden barracks, to be used for a
purpose unknown to us. This was one of the enviable jobs. One
day Bernard was caught picking up a package of food brought
from a Czechoslovak working nearby. The package looked suspicious and a dutiful citizen called the police.

Just as the *Kapo* in charge and the German guard were getting
ready to give Bernard a thorough thrashing, the German carpenter in charge of the whole operation saw what was coming. He
ran over quickly, yelling, "I want that cursed Jew for myself! This
is my territory and my responsibility and I want to teach this swine
a lesson he will never forget. Rest assured he will never dare to
steal again!" A heavy knobbed branch in his hand, he grabbed
Bernard and pulled him into a nearby shed, locking the door
behind him. Quietly he said, "Scream as loud as you possibly can."
Then he proceeded to hit everything in sight, ripped Bernard's
shirt and pants, told him to cry and crawl out on all fours. It
worked like a charm. His skin was saved. It could be done! All one
needed was to come across a man where there were so few men!

In the early, still-dark mornings before we left for work, we
took turns sneaking into the potato shed, grabbing a few potatoes
to bake on the fire in my shop for lunch. One particular morning
it was Romek's turn. While he was inside filling his pockets, someone closed the latch from the outside. I watched the horror as the
double door was pushed desperately from the inside. We were
already lining up for the roll call and he was still stuck inside. We
tried desperately to create diversions to postpone the roll count.
Some made emergency runs to the outhouse; two boys started an
argument. We could not get near the shed to open the door
without alerting the guards. Romek kept pushing with all his
might until somehow, miraculously, the latch gave and the door
sprang open. He barely managed to fall in line in time for the
count. That was the closest of calls. We were devastated and could
not calm down for a long time. There had to be a better way—I
didn't like it at all. We had to find a better way.

In the meantime, we continued our daily marches, some recit-
ing their morning prayers, some theorizing and politicking to
overcome the monotony of the road. Among the new groups that
arrived that summer were some boys no older than eleven. Some

were robust and hardened way above their age. For example, Little David took readily to the hardships. I remember him rolling heavy upright barrels that were loaded with potatoes and quite a few inches taller than himself, with apparent ease. He was always eager to take on any task. He made it and came with us to America. At the same time there was Arnold, an eleven-year-old boy. Equipped with a vocabulary that could make a stevedore blush (a result of growing up during the war), he was still a delicate child. I didn't have a brother and so we grew very close, as he needed help desperately. He marched between Berek and me, and we tried hard to shield him in every way possible. He learned fast and adapted himself to the hardships remarkably well. We became hopeful that Arnold would pull through. But by then, the Moloch of Auschwitz had grown in hunger and efficiency. The S.S. were constantly combing the camps, looking for the weak and sick. One day Arnold caught a cold; too weak to undertake the march to Faülbruck, he remained for the day in the infirmary. When we came home he was gone—sweet, innocent little Arnold. His mother supposedly survived, but I could not face her.

The days grew shorter again, and as we walked we continued to analyze every word, every syllable that reached our ears. We knew history and geography quite well. Names like Baku . . . oil fields . . . Stalingrad. . . . Important, symbolic, they kept recurring in muted conversations around us. Our senses were giving us the message that this is where the decisive battles were being fought. Exciting, but about a thousand miles away. Could this do us any good? Sta-lin-grad, Stalingrad—we listened to the sound and hoped.

The winter of 1942 found us in Faulbrück again, this time for a longer and more eventful stay. Living conditions this second winter in Faulbrück were not much better than the first. The living quarters, with the enormous warehouse practically on the premises, were a little better equipped, thanks to the overflow of unusable items from the army—broken bunks, ripped blankets, damaged pots and pans, and so forth. Those, for us, were items of luxury. Shortages of water and heat caused the most suffering. About January, we got a new civilian administrator (*Lagerführer*) replacing Shaya, who had followed us from Sakrau. The new beast's name was Kiski, and a beast he turned out to be, a butcher by profession and by choice. His reign of terror lasted well over a year. He immediately started to rearrange everything in sight, choosing new *Kapos* who were ruffians, unscrupulous, cruel, and also, for the most part, butchers. Cruelty appealed to Kiski above anything else. Our own *Judenältester* was a fellow by the name of Zehngut—big, mild-mannered and not too smart. He was also vain and terribly selfish, although in his favor, I must admit that his mildness did have a restraining influence in many rough and dangerous moments.

I was employed all over the place in every imaginable capacity, installing new kitchen equipment, lots of plumbing, building partitions, fixing broken locks, windows—you name it. While working on locks, I had to have many keys, so having a feasible excuse, I equipped myself with every master key imaginable. These proved later to be my keys to the kingdom of food. Through some extremely dangerous but richly rewarding forays, they also nearly got me into the kingdom of hell. I believe the main reason I was never caught was that no one would ever guess that I would dare. But more about that later.

In February 1943, Kiski started fishing in our well-known pond behind the complex. As the catch became scarcer by the day, being a butcher, he began to look for other ways to round up the fish. His first idea was to pump out the water. We located a big, used portable pump, which I helped to install, and slowly, over a period of a few days, the pond's water level started to recede. But the fish kept escaping to the deepest pockets of the lake. This made Kiski very angry. One evening, he reached the deepest cavity at the bottom of the lake. The rubber intake hose was not long enough, so we kept lowering the pump as deep as we could. Finally, in slimy half frozen mud, with no end in sight, we left it for the evening. Overnight, the water in that last, deepest hole froze on the surface; next morning, we had to break the ice to submerge the intake valve for further pumping. But in order to empty the water completely, the one-way intake valve on the end of the hose had to be positioned in the deepest spot. It could not be done from the outside. Kiski asked for volunteers who knew how to swim. In February, with a sheet of ice on top—you had to be crazy. And perhaps I was. In any case, I stripped and dove, placed the valve in the deepest spot and ran back to the fireplace in my smithshop to dry. They caught very few fish—hardly any were there. But I caught a middle ear infection, plus an excellent reputation in the eyes of Kiski, as you will see.

This incident took place one week before my mother accidentally arrived at our camp. And one day later, unknown to me then, a girl named Dorka, cute as a button, arrived. In time she would become my wife. As a matter of fact, the first time she laid eyes on me, my head was all bandaged to relieve my pain and help heal my ear infection.

Shlamek, five years old, in Chrzanów, Poland.

Shlamek before the war with his mother, Frieda Gross.

Shlamek (fifth from right) with friends in Chrzanów before the war.

Tamara and Alek Weinreich, both nurses during the typhus epidemic in Gräditz.

Dorka photographed in early 1942 near Sosnowiec, Poland.

Shlamek with his mother and Dorka at the end of 1945.

Dorka and Shlamek married on July 14, 1946 in Munich.

Left to right: Shlamek, David Poltorak (Dorka's cousin), Dorka, Bernard, and Berek, who all lived together after the war. David survived the concentration camp with Shlamek's and Bernard's help.

Romek in 1945.

Mannes Schwarz shortly after the liberation.

Berek Selinger in 1945.

Bernard Moncznik, Dorka's brother, after the war.

Mannes, Dorka, and Shlamek in Hannover shortly before coming to the United States.

Rivka Benczkowska-Levit, who worked in the kitchen of the camp and helped Shlamek and Dorka in time of great need.

6
Spring 1943

1943. The spring of that year brought about the end of the road for most ghettoes in Poland. Step by step, the Germans squeezed the Jewish population out of the living quarters they had occupied all their lives into a concentrated area: a ghetto without walls, confined to a small number of streets, easy to seal off, where the Germans could get their hands on all occupants at a moment's notice. They accomplished their goal; as of March 1943, our town of Chrzanów was declared *Judenrein*, clean of Jews. The balance of the already decimated Jewish population was rounded up. The majority, consisting of old people and children, were taken straight to nearby Auschwitz; the remaining able-bodied few, to labor camps.

My father was already in prison. My mother, then in her 58th year, looked much younger and vigorous, and succeeded in persuading the brutes to select her for work.

For a mother to meet a son in those camps was a very rare event, perhaps one chance in a hundred thousand. In fact, this kind of a reunion was so rare that even the usually heartless guards took notice.

Dorka knew that her brother Bernard was in a place called Faulbrück and tried desperately to be reunited with him. When the final allocation to camps was taking place, Dorka learned to her dismay that she was not going to Faulbrück. The selection was being conducted by a well-known character named Haushield, whom we called the "limping cattle merchant." In desperation, Dorka stepped out of her column, pulled Haushield by the sleeve, and with tears in her eyes, begged him to send her to Faulbrück to her brother. Herr Haushield turned around angrily, then looked and saw the charming little Jewish criminal, her eyes filled with tears. The rock in his chest must have melted for a brief moment. He said in German, *"Du Kleine kommst gleich nach Faulbrück."* (You little one, you go straight to Faulbrück.) And so it was.

On the train journey to their destination, all the girls anxiously questioned the guards, "Are there any men in the camp we are going to?" One of the more talkative told them, "Yes, of course. Only yesterday I witnessed an unusual reunion of a mother and son." They listened, fell silent, and with trepidation in their heart wondered.

Not all women remained in Faulbrück. Some were sent further on to surrounding camps. But keeping Mother and Dorka with us presented no great difficulty. Kiski, while making the selection, was told by Zehngut, "This is the mother of the Techniker." *"Die bleibt hier"* (She stays here), he barked. The freezing dive had paid off. Because Dorka's brother was well liked, she also had no problem remaining with us.

These two eventful days turned out to be important turning points in my life. To begin with, I had to give up an idea that had been taking shape in my mind for some time—the idea of running. After carefully weighing all the pros and cons, my decision had been firm. I was not going to wait any longer and face the certainty of becoming a sitting duck. . . . With Berek or alone, I was going to take my chance and break out shortly before harvest time. I planned to move southeast, walking nights only, hiding and sleeping in the fields during the daytime. I would head toward Czechoslovakia, Hungary, Rumania. About 350 miles. . . . It had been done before. There was a chance. But with my mother's arrival I had to forget it for now. But then, one never recognizes a blessing in disguise. . . .

During the days that followed, we had no time for reflecting. Everyone had to make adjustments. Mother adapted fairly well to the chores and demands of the kitchen, glad to have found me, but sad and worried about Father.

There was no recourse. We had to make the best of what we had, and keep in mind that circumstances could have been a lot worse. . . . At least we did not have to live in the immediate shadow of the chimneys! We knew little then about the extent of those horrors. We had only a vague inkling; we saw the lightning, we heard the thunder, but we were not aware that the storm was already raging full force. Listening to the sad and horrid tales of the two years since we left home, we were anxious to get back and be absorbed by our daily routines. This helped to take our minds off the looming, imminent dark dangers, and push such thoughts into a far corner of our minds.

To give you an example of our reactions and the extent of our ignorance concerning the ongoing genocide, let me recount an episode that took place about a year later. At that time, Lehman and his second in command, Liszek, were our new *Lagerführers,* in Gräditz, having taken over after we managed to outlive Kiski. They were both decadent but nice enough fellows. They needed to appear one Monday before noon at an important conference of S.S. bigshots. Their car, a Hanomag (the forerunner of today's BMW), had not been functioning properly for some time, and because they were afraid to take a chance of missing the conference, they called on our great expert Altschul (about whom you will hear much more later) to install a new engine. Altschul, with his stiff leg, was unable to get under the car himself, so I took his place and he guided my hands throughout the whole operation.

Without hydraulic lift or tunnel, with the most primitive of equipment, we managed to remove the old engine and install the new one. We started on Friday afternoon, worked through the night, then all day Saturday, and through the second night, into Sunday morning—approximately forty hours in total. It took extra long, because when the new engine was installed we found that the suspension did not line up properly and had to do it over again. By Sunday morning, my eyes kept closing. I could not resist sleep any longer. Altschul kept putting cold, wet rags on my forehead to keep me going. When we finally finished I fell asleep under the shower, but we put them on the road on time. They were happy and rewarded us well.

But the point of my story is this: while lying unnoticed under the car I overheard the following exchange between Lehman and Liszek.

"Hm! Der Techniker."

"He is a diligent fellow, a talented young chap. What a shame he will have to wind up in the furnace."

"Ja eine Schande (Ah, what a shame!)"

Listening to the matter-of-fact statement of the foregone conclusion, my blood froze. But only for a short while. "Stay away, you frightening thoughts!" At this moment my stomach was full; my spirits were filled with defiance. I thought, "You can wait! That will never happen to me!" After they left, we siphoned off another gallon of gas into our standby, awful looking jalopy, which we made sure to keep in good running condition.

Back to Faulbrück, however, and our adjustments to the new

circumstances, trying hard to keep constantly the ever-present feeling of dark panic at bay.

Dorka

Our romance had strange beginnings. Dorka was not yet fifteen, very shy and very proud; I, more mature and quite fresh. The first time we spoke was at a well. While she was fetching a pail of water, the chain broke and the pail fell to the bottom. I climbed it, got it out easily, and handed it to her. Addressing her face to face I said, "Next time you be careful. I might not be so close by." She blushed, said, "Thank you, Sir," *(Dziękuje panu)* turned around and walked away, bending under the weight of the heavy pail of water. A force as strong as gravity kept pulling me in the direction of the potato peeling room where she was working. I wanted to get her attention, but did not know her name, so I threw a potato peel at her back. She turned around angrily as I said, "Well, how are you, madam?" *(Jak się pani ma).* All I got was a dirty look. I tried a potato peel again the next day, explaining that unless she told me her name, this was the only way I could contact her. "What for?" she asked, but gave me her name.

With her brother Bernard's help, we started communicating a little more easily. Once, I happened to be inside the supply house fixing a broken window when Dorka passed by below. Inside the supply room, I was surrounded by stacks of butter bars, dried fruit packages, and lots of other goodies. My iron rule for such an opportunity was never to take anything I could not swallow. But this time, with Dorka passing by, and no one in sight, it seemed an unusual opportunity. I could not pass this one up. I whistled to attract her attention and threw one bar of butter out the window. Blushing and bewildered, with horror in her eyes, she looked up at me with a questioning motion: "Where can I put it?" I pointed to her decolletage. If I had been within reach or if eyes could kill, this would have turned out to be my last bit of mischief! Eventually, however, left with no choice, she had to take my advice. Thereafter, for some time, she avoided me like a plague, but I persevered.

Summer came and passed. The days took on a different meaning as we grew closer. The song of the lark filled the air; the blood in my veins was turning sweet and the desire to live increased a hundredfold.

Years later in America a friend once asked Dorka, "I heard Sam call you different names. What is your actual name?" Smiling, Dorka replied: "In Poland they called me 'Zydowka' (coarse for Jewess). The Germans yelled 'Jude.' In concentration camp I became a 'Häftling' (prisoner). Love notes, in order to protect my identity, I received under 'Zosia' (Sofie).

"After liberation my title was 'D.P.' (displaced person). In America I was a 'Greener' (Greenhorn). Now I am a survivor. . . . Doris is my actual name, I love it! And no more changes, please!"

I still call her Dorka.

The face of the war began to change. We heard of defeats—El Alamein, Stalingrad—air raids . . . finally, American involvement. The Germans were slowed, even stopped in some instances. Nothing, however, stopped or even slowed them in their progress toward our destruction. On the contrary, visits of the S.S. to our camps became more frequent. No one dared to stay in the infirmary. As long as you could move, you went to work. We kept losing people—both sick and healthy; Auschwitz needed fodder and a workforce, too. Around summer of 1943, two strange deaths occurred in Faulbrück. Two girls, Itka Kerenkraut from Chrzanów and a German girl named Lina, took sick and after a few days, just slipped away. In view of the prevailing hygienic conditions, typhus was immediately suspected. The cattle merchant Haushield happened to be visiting the camp and confronted our Dr. Haar with the question, "Do you think it's typhus? Should I bring our own doctor?" Haar looked him straight in the eyes and said, "No. They died of pneumonia." I do not know how positive he was that it wasn't typhus, but I am certain that he knew they did not die of pneumonia.

Dr. Haar

"Herr Lagerführer, I am a doctor, not a *Kapo*."

This was Dr. Haar's reply when ordered by Kiski to beat up an inmate. Everyone froze. His skin and position were on the line. Kiski blinked and walked away.

A man who strongly desired, and mostly succeeded, to give the impression of being an unsentimental rogue, Dr. Haar's compassion and decency were deeply hidden from all who professed to know him. He also succeeded in making many hate him. As far as the inmates were concerned, he had to be stern and sometimes even cruel, often for their own protection. Because of that he was accused by some of taking bribes, though personally I do not believe it. He was closer than anyone to the German administration, and therefore the *Kapos* and company tried to be obsequiously friendly, mostly out of fear. And he managed to keep that fear alive.

But no matter what he did or how he behaved, he certainly saved us all from instant destruction, risking his neck in the process! The typhus bacillus must have indeed been present. It remained dormant for about five or six more months, then it exploded full force in Gräditz. However, thanks to Haar's statement, we were left alone. Later, when the epidemic broke, it was too risky and too late to move us anywhere, so we stayed quarantined, and at least half of us managed to survive.

If a German doctor had suspected typhus in the beginning, we all would have been on trucks to Auschwitz the next day. Fortunately for us, the Germans trusted Dr. Haar. I further suspect that Kiski and company had some apprehensions and set about to move us, this time permanently, into the much more concentrated and compact quarters of Gräditz. They did not want to lose their domain, either.

At this point, we were nearing 1,700 inmates—all of us crammed in the four stories of an old mill, somewhere between sixty and eighty thousand square feet of space. A true snake pit!

By then my reputation as a handyman/troubleshooter was well-established and Kiski, with Zehngut, decided to put me in charge of the sewers and water supply. Although I did not have to go outside to work, my tasks were not something to be envied. Washing facilities were nonexistent. In previous years, we had used the few faucets on the ground floor next to the sty barn. For 400 to 500 men, it had to suffice; but 1,700 was a different matter. To start with, I installed a few shower heads, many more faucets, and long wash-up sinks. I was confronted daily with about 1,600 men needing to wash at the same time. It was sheer bedlam. Many were angry, holding me responsible when the faucets ran dry. And could anyone blame them? Final deterioration always starts when you stop cleaning yourself. Many did not even try to get under the cold shower or cold water to wash their faces and bodies, but those who wanted, and water was not available, suffered and were understandably angry. I was in a terrible predicament; we had only one well which, under the most favorable circumstances, like rain and moist weather, could only deliver enough for the needs of 800 people. I was desperate. Necessity drove me to take an incalculable risk.

Next to our washroom was the barn. The cattle got their water from another well further down in the village. Constructing a maze of pipes to camouflage my scheme, I coupled two pipes to siphon water from the cattle's well into our own. A plumber could have detected it in less than a minute; the additional danger was that in our own well, the pump that fed us was submerged about seven feet below the surface, so the siphoning of additional water had to be stopped before it rose high enough to flood our own pump. I had to run out in the middle of the night to check the water level and stop the flow before disaster struck. Lack of sleep made me confide in Altschul, who miraculously constructed a makeshift automatic float, an ingenious contraption that gave me a chance to get some sleep. All of this activity had to take place during the night so that the spring had time to replenish the well by morning, otherwise the cattle would have died of thirst.

No one except Altschul knew about my undertaking. A number of times I overheard conversations between Kiski and Zuhr, with Herr Zuhr complaining, "In all the years in Gräditz, I've never encountered a water problem. I wonder what causes it now?" Each time I listened, my heart would pound like mad. Then I would refrain for a while, until the next shortage. But it was no use; it had to be done. I was lucky that most plumbers were away fighting the Russians. This practice continued until I succumbed to typhus myself. Thereafter, for the half of us who survived, there was no need to steal water anymore.

How Low Can a Man Sink?

Among other things, the outhouse was also my responsibility. Keeping it clean and emptying it in time kept me busy for many hours every week. The only tool I had at my disposal was a hand-operated seesaw pump. To use it I had to wait for the local peasants to come with their receptacles and get their precious cargo. Now even the fear of catching any of our diseases would stop them from claiming a free gift.

One evening while on my routine inspection I noticed a solo visitor, an emaciated wretch of a man sitting on the balustrade and holding underneath him a small cardboard box with one hand. Clearly he was trying to intercept something before it went down the open pit.

"What in the world are you doing?" I asked. "Last night," he replied, "while chewing on a piece of bread I swallowed my last tooth. It had a gold cap on it. I am desperately trying to find it. I have no more strength left, I hoped to get a loaf of bread for it and now it's gone. What am I going to do?" I hope he found it. I never saw him again.

During the second half of 1943 I engaged in a lot of stealing or, as we called it, "organizing." I must have truly been watched over by a lucky star. My days were spent inside the Gräditz camp working on everything imaginable, and getting to know, in the process, every hidden corner of the mill. I detected many possibilities for "organizing" some extra food. All carried a serious element of danger. By that time, besides Mother and Dorka, I was sharing my spoils with about ten more friends. Knowing I was needed plus a sense of responsibility gave me encouragement and kept me going. Perhaps another element was a hidden quest for adventure that pushed me sometimes beyond the limits of reason.

Next to the right side of the mill was a lovely little orchard studded with pear and apple trees. The two windows of the mill facing it had vertical iron bars about seven inches apart. Spreading two of them a trifle, I managed to squeeze through and lower myself ten feet down, into the orchard. Once there I climbed a tree and filled my pouch with fruits, then hooked it onto a rope that hung down from the window, and signaled my companion to pull it back up. Quite simple—except for a few complications.

One was the constant traffic of inmates to the washroom. The window I used was in a small cell, next to the washroom entrance, that served as an overnight morgue for those unfortunates who would be buried the next morning. Before the advent of typhus, when mountains of corpses piled up, the Jewish ritual of cleansing the dead was strictly adhered to and water had to be made available. Full credit for performing that task goes to my friend Moyshe Buxbaum. If he had not himself been overcome by typhus, no corpse would have been buried without cleansing, no matter how many there were.

Only on nights when there was an occupant in the morgue could I visit the garden undisturbed. And even then, we sometimes had surprises. Once a courageous fellow inmate managed to follow us, demanding a ransom of a few apples in exchange for not reporting us. We called his bluff, and watched him walk up to the very entrance to the police station before we lost our nerve and paid up. I must admit I couldn't blame him, because this was probably his only opportunity in a long time to get some extra food.

Another night, as I lowered myself into the orchard, car lights burned from the street straight in my direction. The car pulled up so close to where I hit the ground that the beam of light shone right above my head, so that I was not noticed. My ticker stopped and so did my breathing; I saw myself being next in line to the morgue. The lights went off, the door opened just to the right above my head, and out came Kiski, luckily turning toward the back of the car, thus avoiding stepping on my head. Out from the other side came Grätel, Zuhr's younger daughter.

Frozen into the ground, I was not sure which way the all-in-flames couple would roll. Afraid to breathe, I lay there quietly. Grateful for the moment that they had not wound up on top of me, I had to listen to every detail of the episode. It seemed endless—a porno movie for the blind. If I had been found, Kiski would have had to dispose of me. His wife lived on the premises and he did not need any witnesses. Indeed, life and death were in very close proximity. But my luck held and I escaped once more.

Kiski's car and motorcycle were my responsibility. The beneficial aspect of this was that I always knew when he was away; the bad part was that in the beginning I had no experience with cars except in how to keep them clean. One afternoon Kiski returned with a flat tire, yelled, "Techniker!" pointed to the flat and said, "Fix it! I am leaving tomorrow morning."

My only experience with flat tires was patching bicycle tubes, so I removed the wheel, and proceeded to wedge the inner tire out with a small crowbar. It was my first try; by the time I got the tube out, I'd punched an additional six holes into it. When I submerged it in water, I broke out in a cold sweat as I counted seven separate sets of bubbles. Embarrassed and petrified, I had to glue on seven patches.

At this time I first met Altschul. A truly rare and eccentric character, he was born in Czechoslovakia and had lived in France. Supposedly he was the chief electrical engineer of the Paris airport. By now he was in his fifties; one leg was completely stiff, but he was exceptionally knowledgeable in the fields of electricity and automobiles. On this particular day he had just returned from work and was in no hurry to clean up—as a matter of fact, Altschul was never in a hurry to clean up. He watched me sweat and smiled. "Don't worry," he said. "It's no problem." Assisted by his wonderful expertise, we glued the patches on quickly and efficiently and put the tire back. I washed the car; he let it run and adjusted the engine. Next morning, Kiski smiled as he drove away. Thank you, Altschul! I thought, and I knew I would be returning to him again and again.

That same day, with Kiski away, I made my first foray into his domain. Most of the mill's windows were located in the staircase shaft, all facing the center court. The only two additional windows, also facing the center court, were in a room located near the separate entrance to the women's quarters. In that room, Kiski kept special supplies meant for the German administration . . . sugar, cereals, rice, beans, blocks of butter, lard for cooking, plus a number of other delicacies—delicacies we had forgotten the looks of. With my set of keys, entering presented no problem. The windows facing the court assured me that no one had driven in and no one was on his way up to the first floor. On this job, I worked solo to be absolutely sure to stick to my rules—not to take anything that could be counted, or to take too much and be noticed. I continued doing this for a few months. All my safety precautions practically assured my not being caught in the act. Nevertheless, this was the most fearful of all my escapades: every squeak of the floor, every little noise, plus the fear of a frame-up, terrified me constantly. I learned then never to judge or envy a burglar. I wished we would move again, or that some other excuse would force me to stop. And I didn't have to wait long to get my wish.

One Sunday morning, instead of letting us rest as usual, we were called for a line-up in the Appellplatz. After we had stood waiting for quite a while, Zehngut appeared in his white golf sweater and shining boots, with Kiski next to him, and made an announcement. "Somebody has visited the *Lagerführer's* warehouse. A few packages of butter are missing. If it is one of you (apparently he was not certain), we expect you to find the culprit. If you don't and this happens again, the whole camp will get food only every second day. Dismissed!"

You can imagine what went through my mind while listening to him. I am fairly certain by now that I know what happened. A fellow who was a locksmith by profession either followed me, or found his way on his own, got in and stupidly (perhaps luckily for me) took the only item that could be counted.

One should not wonder about or misunderstand our obsession and paranoia on the subject of food. The first weeks in Gräditz taught us a lesson. We learned firsthand how severe hunger really feels. Guided by that experience, every one of us made endless efforts and took great risks not to be left without any reserves, however small, of something extra to eat.

Experiences like this one and the incident previously mentioned, when one of us got stuck inside the shed, made me search constantly for safer methods. On the roof of the mill stood a large, round water tank, abandoned and forgotten, full of dirt, mold, and slime. This looked to me like a wonderful, safe storage place. We climbed the broken ladder leading to the top, and suspended two old knapsacks on a rope deep down into the tank. Even if someone were by accident to come onto the roof, they would never pay any attention to an old mud-covered, half-torn rope.

Now that we had a perfect, empty hiding place, all we needed was to fill it. The big shed where the large loads of potatoes were stored stood next to the mill house. If we lowered a rope perpendicularly from the roof, the end would come down right in front of the entrance to the potato shed. I made sure that all hinges and locks were well oiled so that they did not make a sound while being opened. On dark nights, two of us would wait for the guard on duty to march to the opposite end of the yard. Once we were out of his sight, we would quickly make our entrance into the shed. Inside, we lay low until the guard reached our end again; then, when he resumed his return march, we pulled on the hanging rope as a signal to send down the first empty knapsack. On the chance that we might be intercepted on the way to the job, we carried nothing with us except a piece of rusty bent wire, which was the actual key.

Quietly we would fill the first sack, send it up, and get the next one down. This operation went like clockwork for about six months without any serious hitches. Once the key fell out of my hand and got mixed up with the potatoes. I was ready to leave it there, but my companion that night had more patience and would not stop searching through the potatoes in the dark until he found it.

Another time we had to turn back, because one of the fellows whose turn it was to accompany me that night had too weak a stomach and would not go through with it. I must admit that despite all the precautions we took, it was a scary proposition. We even went so far as to create a blackout while the activity was taking place. Romek stood in the meter room watching that the light should not go on before we were safely back under our covers, seemingly fast asleep.

Cooking all our loot was the next big problem. Altschul taught us how to construct ultraflat hot plates. Whenever and wherever the occasion arose, we would pull out the heating spirals from small hotplates or get hold of broken and abandoned ones. We flattened the spirals in a vise, and Altschul supplied thin sheets of transparent, heat-resistance insulation. We stuck the flattened spirals in between the sheets, let two ends stick out, and whenever we found ourselves near an electric outlet, we were ready to cook a hot meal. We called them "hot books" because we kept them in our pockets, folded like a notebook. What a blessing they were!

The Dutch Jews

Meanwhile, new arrivals kept being brought to Gräditz. For the first time, several groups of Dutch Jews now joined us.

The Dutch Jews had many more opportunities to escape Hitler than we had—yet they did not. Those delicate, sweet, amiable souls—how quickly they succumbed! At the time when transports of Dutch Jews arrived in Gräditz, some of us easterners had already been incarcerated for three years. Having spent all our lives in poor environments with very few comforts, always surrounded by Polish neighbors filled with envy and hate, our hides had had to develop a toughness merely to exist, even in normal times. The Dutch Jews, on the other hand, enjoyed both physical and mental luxury. Then, all of a sudden, they found themselves in Gräditz. They were no match for their deprived brethren: they lacked stamina and self-control under duress; they had no tolerance for pain. They caved in so rapidly that it was unbearable to watch.

Remembering the Dutch Jews raises again the nagging questions: How? . . . Why? After many years of contemplation, I am convinced that the most obvious and overwhelming reason for our destruction was expendability. We were *expendable*. The whole world could get along easily and well without us. Consequently, we were first in line to be sacrificed in the process of defeating Hitler, an ugly thought, perhaps, but unfortunately true. I do not condone the world's behavior, but knowing history, I cannot fully condemn it either. I have not yet found any examples of noble efforts, let alone sacrifices, of one people trying to save another.

The fault and therefore the guilt were primarily our own. We could not afford to continue living the way we lived. By repeatedly failing to see this in time, we paid the price. During those horrible years in that man-made hell where we could clearly see the consequences of complacency, we still did not learn our lesson. Man is a complex animal; he is superb in forgetting, especially pain. (Supposedly, if a woman would remember birth pains, no children would ever be born again.)

The Dutch were mostly professionals: doctors, teachers, musicians, one sailor, a few mechanics. Some were members of the Dutch National Symphony Orchestra. One such was Mr. Haas, a talented violinist, extremely tall with a long, sad face and melancholy eyes. I remember him fondly from the time when I was lying half alive, reawakening from the murderous typhus fever. I had the rare luxury of sharing with my friend Berek a double bunk in the cubicle of the furnace room where I worked. Through the swinging saloon-like doors, Haas's face and part of his violin would appear. He knew I loved to listen to Tosseli's aria for violin, to Schubert, Debussy, Brahms, Bach. He smiled gently as he played, happy to give. His violin helped me back to life. He had just recovered from typhus himself, and the voracious appetite that followed that sickness was killing him quickly. By the time I got on my feet, he was already gone. Gentle Mr. Haas.

One outstanding exception to the Dutch passivity was the sailor. Fierce looking, his eyes were always full of angry defiance. Suddenly one day, like an unexpected electric shock, the news came that the Dutch sailor and a companion had escaped. A couple of days passed. We thought he might have had outside connections and support; perhaps he had made it. We expected repercussions. Another day passed. Then, at night, they brought the pair back. Kiski now showed the full force of his sadistic bestiality—he supposedly ran them over a few times with his car. Our *Kapos* took advantage of the opportunity to show Kiski their capabilities in a night of true sadistic orgy. Myself? I did my best to stay away. Hiding, fearful of being asked by Kiski to participate in the carnage, I went as far as cracking a water main to create an emergency that had to be taken care of immediately. It wasn't necessary; I was not called.

After the killings, their bodies were left hanging for hours on the Appellplatz as a warning to us all.

A few months later, there was another attempt to escape, this time by a childhood friend of mine, Moniek Ruff. He lived across the street, and many hours of our youth were spent conversing across the narrow street. We did our homework together and talked politics . . . girls, and so forth. Window to window we played a game of recognizing passing cars by sound—Chevrolets, Buicks, Tatra, Polish, Fiat, Skoda. We got so good at it that we rarely made a mistake.

That was in the early 1930s. Moniek managed to stay home until the last deportation in the spring of 1943. He could not adapt to the hardships of Gräditz and constantly walked around with the idea of escaping. I tried hard to talk him out of it—to no avail. No questions were asked. It was a tacit understanding—what you don't know, torture cannot make you reveal.

The evening of the planned escape arrived. He came to say goodbye. I shared with him my few Deutsche marks and tried once more to convince him of the futility of his plan. The few of us who knew waited with great tension, but unfortunately, not too long. The next morning, Moniek and his three companions were picked up at the railroad station in the next village even before any alarm sounded in our camp. After a bloody beating, they were all taken to Auschwitz. So much for the attempts to escape.

Can a fish escape the net? Our chances against the net were no better than that of a small fish on dry soil.

I will question forever why our great sages, the likes of Jochanan Ben Zakai, didn't think about a military academy at least half as much as about the Yeshiva. That it does not take long to develop an efficient and valiant military force, Jews proved beyond doubt in 1967, only a short twenty years after our humiliation.

However, in 1943 we were still in Gräditz. When the Dutch sailor and his companions escaped, they were hung for display on high poles with strong light above them. We had erected those poles shortly before this tragic event, and I remember it well because those poles were indirectly responsible for what I considered to be the luckiest day of my life.

In the same transport that brought my mother came a fellow from our town named Jankiel Mandelbaum. Before the war, he had manufactured candy, and all of us youngsters remembered him fondly. He was also the man who brought me the awful news of my father's death by torture in the prison of Myslowice. Ironically, my father had been arrested because of mistaken identity— the Gestapo were looking for his cousin, who stayed out of sight, survived the war, and lived in Israel until 1988.

Mr. Mandelbaum did not adapt well to the Gräditz hardships. He suffered terribly, dragged along for two or three months, and finally came to the end of his powers. One morning he refused to get up. He remained in bed, resigned to whatever would happen. Kiski made his stand. He wanted to make clear to everyone what awaited those who refused to get up and go to work.

Fortunately for me, on the morning of this sorrowful day, the village electrician, a decent elderly fellow, took six of us to a forest to chop down a couple of trees to make poles for the large spotlights to be installed in our Appellplatz. We spent most of the day cutting down and pruning three healthy, strong, and straight fifteen-footers. When we finally arrived back home, I knew immediately that something had gone wrong. If anyone still had any doubts as to whether Kiski was capable of murder, the events of that day proved it. My helper in the furnace room, who always pinch-hit for me during my absence or while I was doing other odd jobs, relayed to me the whole terrifying story. Kiski had had

Mr. Mandelbaum tied to a bench, face up, covered him with blankets, and ordered my helper and another man to pour boiling water continuously on top of the blankets until the horrible convulsions of the choking man stopped. I came back in time to remove his dead body and could not help but see his face, gruesomely distorted from choking. His twisted hands, his horrifying features remained vividly with me for a very long time. I will forever be immensely grateful to my lucky star that I was not confronted with having to make the choice to participate or suffer the consequences.

The News Changes

It took us a long time to regain our equilibrium after this kind of an event. The power of the will to live eventually won and we continued, cheered a little more often now by news of heavy bombing of cities and numerous Wehrmacht defeats. Despite the fear of being victimized in revenge for the Allied bombings, we could not wait to get more of such news. Mischievous Altschul used to whistle, wink and say, "Hey . . . do you want to hear the news? Get the boys!"

He would sit down in the garage, take a specially prepared steel plate, rub it with his magic piece of wire, and less than a half a minute later, the scream would come from upstairs, "Techniker! *(Das verfluchte scheis radio is wieder kapputt)*. The damned radio went berserk again!" I would jump up to take it for repairs, then would set up a chain of sentries and listen. Too bad that most of the news broadcasts were in English—among us, we spoke every Slavic language, and Altschul spoke French, but not one of us knew a word of English. Once in a while, we caught the French underground broadcast. It was exciting, but most of the news we already knew, and it did not pay to risk our lives.

The Barter System at Gräditz

The law of supply and demand still ruled. Business and barter transactions were conducted on many levels for many different items. Everything had a price: two bowls of soup for one ration of bread; for three to six cigarettes, one could get a slice of bread, butter or jam. One could buy a shirt, trousers, shoes. I myself was buying silver spoons—a small one for one bread ration, a big one for two. This was the raw material with which I later produced jewelry items. Strange though it may seem, once we managed to get through the initial inspection, before entering the compound of a camp, without being detected, our small hidden possessions were fairly safe. We were still allowed to keep our clothing and without extraordinary cause were not searched. Among the 1,700 inmates, a few were lucky enough to hold onto their heirlooms—a gold watch, a ring, a gold coin, and other tiny valuables.

For a while, our camp at Gräditz was amply supplied with the luxury called bread, though very few knew why. Romek was at that time the Gräditz dentist. The village butcher and the baker were great friends of Kiski, so Romek was given permission to work on their teeth. Taking advantage of the contact, we took a chance to let the baker know that he might be able to pick up a nice gold pocket watch in exchange for some bread. He was already supplying a few thousand loaves every month. He immediately showed keen interest and asked how much. I must admit, personally I would never have had the temerity to ask for so high a number, but "200," said Romek. A pittance for the baker, an indescribable fortune for us.

At this particular time, the most one could get for a gold pocket watch was seven loaves, and then he had to bribe the *Kapo* to help him smuggle them into the camp, where they were not too safe either. We, on the other hand, offered twenty-five loaves, delivered under the seller's pillow at intervals suiting him best. We never dealt with the seller directly for safety reasons, but had a couple of intermediaries to whom we paid a commission, also in bread. We could easily afford it. There is no better deal than one in which both parties are fully satisfied.

The owners of the watches had only one regret, that they did not have one more to sell. This went on for a couple of months, until the full outbreak of typhus and the ensuing quarantine. To hand over the loaves to the seller was simple; to take in hundreds of loaves of bread was a very dangerous and complicated matter. Our blessing in disguise this time was the stupidity of our otherwise ignorant and brutal butcher/cook. He was utterly incapable of distinguishing between 1,000 and 1,200 loaves—I doubt whether his capacity for counting went beyond twenty. The girl he had his eye on was in on the deal, and she knew how to make sure that he never got near us during deliveries.

The most rewarding part of this undertaking was the fact that, during that period in Gräditz, no one was interested in an extra bowl of soup. Supply and demand proved to be truly in control.

We always dreaded the thought of moving and the difficult process of acclimatization. Once we were settled in one place for a while, most of the inmates found ways to help themselves either through contacts with German foremen or prisoners-of-war of other nationalities, or by risking their skin and going for broke, often recklessly. Sometimes too recklessly: for example, one reckless guy removed a reserve transmission leather belt from an ammunition factory. Luckily, the French P.O.W.s were blamed. Leather was as rare as diamonds—it was absolutely unavailable to civilians. A pair of shoe soles bought easily a couple of loaves of bread. Another book would have to be written to list all the tricks we used. This, however, was the only resistance we could resort to and we never stopped using it, no matter how dangerous!

During my years in camp, I met many men I did not like. But I never met a man who did not like Bernard, Dorka's brother. His smiling face, his ever readiness to help ingratiated him with many, including the Germans, even the toughest ones. At that time we had a new cook named Matchky—a mean character. Bernard helped out in the kitchen. One day, Matchky caught him passing some sugar to the infirmary for a couple of his sick friends and from that day on, made his life absolutely miserable. Afraid of losing his job, Bernard resorted to showing off his only possession left from home, a silver pocketwatch. It worked. In the beginning, Matchky didn't want to take the watch, but Bernard reassured him that it was a burden for him to hide it each night. Eventually, he said, it would be stolen anyhow. This persuasion worked. From that point on, Matchky's attitude turned around one hundred and eighty degrees. To top it off, he put Bernard in charge of feeding his gigantic black dog.

As I have mentioned, the kitchen was at the entrance to the square court. The doghouse was behind the camp, about two hundred feet away. The morsels left for the dog could surely have fed a dozen inmates. Well, as you can imagine, Bernard did not deliver the whole meal to the dog. I watched, and could not believe my eyes: we all had a big laugh watching the dog getting skinny and Bernard getting fatter. It soon became too obvious. Eventually Matchky noticed the change, called Bernard over, and with fury declared, "From now on I will feed the dog myself. *(Du verfluchter Jude)*!" I am convinced that the pocketwatch saved Bernard's bones from being broken to pieces.

Romek and I had a unique and enviable position in Gräditz. Most important, we never had to take part in inflicting mistreatment or cruelites against our fellow prisoners. While we could not please everybody, in many instances we managed to be helpful. Those facts and our close contacts with the German authorities kept many—especially the *Kapos* and even Zehngut—guessing with some apprehension as to whether we were not in some way bribing someone and even having a decision-making influence. This circumstance suited us just fine. It kept the monkeys off our backs for good, and while they were angry that we did not bow and pay them homage, they were also afraid to antagonize us and just lay in waiting. This was especially true of one character named Kuba Kosenzweig, a deranged raving lunatic, who could not control his animalism while meting out punishmnts. Kiski loved his performances.

At this time I was heavily engaged in installing additional water line connections to improve on the terribly inadequate washroom facilities. One bright morning Kiski sent me across the street to the village butcher, who had no water. My heart stopped beating for a second. I knew the problem, of course—they shared Zuhr's well. The constant draining I conducted had brought the water level below the one-way valve too frequently, and dried the leather disk that kept the water in the suction pipe, thus causing the loss of the prime. All I had to do was replace the leather disk, and reprime the pump. My guess proved to be right; with good cheer, and fairly sure of myself, I made what turned out to be a very foolish remark. Half jokingly I asked them, *"Was gibt es wen is wasser gibt?"* (Can I expect something nice if I get your water back right away?) The butcher's wife smilingly nodded her head, then apparently went straight to Kiski to ask his advice on how to reward me.

In the meantime having fixed the well, I forgot about it, and went back to my work. By noon, with Romek standing next to me, I was busy connecting two pieces of tubing, when a sudden powerful kick in the back sent me tumbling over the pipe, my head hitting the wall in front of me. I managed to open one eye and to my greatest surprise, saw Kiski in a rage, now working over Romek, then back to me. I saw it all in a flash! . . . he had found out my water scheme, and this would be the end of me! Through his clenched teeth, he said, "I am not through with you yet. I will show you what you will get for bringing the water back," then left us reeling in pain and walked away. (Despite the pain, I was relieved that it was not the water scheme.) Half an hour later Zehngut told us to be on the *Appellplatz* when all the inmates would file in after work. As you might correctly guess, we were not to be envied. Zehngut would not talk. Dr. Haar told us only that there would be floggings. Kuba Rozenzweig's prayers had been answered. I also imagine that all those who envied us (without malice) chuckled a little.

I must say, that contrary to the accepted physical law that time does not stand still—for us, that afternoon, it did! Only pleasant hours pass quickly. . . . After what seemed like ages of agonized waiting, the dreadful moment finally came. We had to pull our trousers down and bend over in full view of the whole camp to receive five smacks each with Kuba's famous leather whip. Only five? Probably in recognition of past services performed, I thought. However, the executioner was Kuba, an expert in inflicting pain. While his orders were five each, no one told him how quickly to strike the blows. The ten hits were delivered very slowly, with intervals in between long enough that you could faint and be revived again. We thought it would never end, but eventually, as everything must, it did. In the aftermath, while we writhed in pain, Dr. Haar made fun of my delicate flesh. For weeks, I had the most colorful pattern on my behind, worthy of being copied on canvas by any abstract painter deserving of the name.

The sitting position was out for about six weeks. Kuba must have been remorseful—he hung himself right after liberation. But Kiski boasted to the baker in the village, "Today I let my two best Jews have it."

7

The Typhus Epidemic

We were coming ever closer to the final disaster at Gräditz: undeniable cases of typhus kept popping up with increasing frequency. We trembled, fearing evacuation. Finally, inevitably, the lingering epidemic exploded with a fury, aided by lice, filth, and totally inadequate hygienic conditions. Fortunately, Kiski was gone by then and the team of Lehman and Lishek loved their new domain enough to do everything in their power to maintain it. By then too many of us were sick and dying to make an evacuation feasible. Lehman and Lishek must have persuaded the higher-ups to resort to a quarantine. About a month before the disease had spread significantly, they took all female inmates under thirty years of age who were employed in the village of Peterswaldau's ammo factory to a new location—the old castle called Zwanziger. Among them was Dorka. We lost contact.

Typhus now raged in full force. Many inmates fell like trees, the big ones first. Young, vigorous fellows would suffer two to three days of extremely high fever and a couple more days of hallucination, then fade away. There were no medications; two doctors; three male nurses, Alek Weinreich, and two devoted Dutchmen; Dr. Brown and his brother; and one female nurse, Tamara, for more than a thousand sick people. Despite their superhuman effort, they could hardly help. The corpses piled up in the staircase shaft much faster than they could be buried. Internally, we had freedom to the point that on Passover the still devout managed to clean and set aside one kettle in the kitchen strictly: "Kosher for Passover." The Germans were afraid to come near us. Garlic was supposed to be some kind of defense; I ate more of it during the couple of weeks I waited for the disease to hit me than during all my life. One night I returned it and that was it. I had prepared myself as much as possible.

As I mentioned before, I had squeezed a double bunk for

Berek and myself into the little room. On the ledge, I put up two containers of liquid with a rubber pipe at the bottom and a valve at the end of the pipe—to speak plainly, an old-fashioned enema. Too weak to hold a cup in our hands, we had only to open the valve and drink. Sometimes we were too weak to close it again and lost all the water. Bernard, who had had typhus before while in Russia, on duty laying tracks for the Wehrmacht in the winter of 1941, kept refilling our water supply. But being among the few left on their feet, he did not know who to attend to first. All I remember was seeing Dorka's worried face, floating by strangely once in awhile, so I was never alone. I had another head next to me on the pillow all the time—strange feeling: there were two of me! I do not know how many days it lasted.

As the fury of the fever began to subside, I tried to get out of bed and found, to my horror, that my knees down to my feet did not exist, they were completely powerless. I tried to get up, and fell right back into bed. For a long time, getting up, standing, and walking, especially on stairs, were completely out of the question. Berek, above me, did not fare much better, and had an even harder time coming down from the top bunk.

Later came the voracious appetite, an aftermath of the sickness. Had we not lost about half of our numbers, we would surely all have died from hunger. Because the dead were unaccounted for, our food situation got a lot better for a while. You want to save the world from starvation? Simple solution—kill half of it. . . .

Mother took sick a few days after I did. She was sixty years old. According to statistics, for people over fifty, the chance of surviving typhus is one in a million. She was delirious for a long time. I was already on my feet and the epidemic seemed to be losing its fury. Dr. Haar, who somehow managed to postpone his own bout (though he paid for it later; he was sick for a very long time and lost his eyesight temporarily), looked at mother and only shook his head. "No way," his eyes were saying. She lingered on and woke up for awhile, hallucinated, asked me to move her shoes closer to her bed, and fell back on her pillow. Everyone thought, "This is the end." I ran down into the courtyard where I encountered Liszek.

He looked at me, doubting whether it was really the Techniker who had kept his motorcycle and all else in order. I walked over to him and said, "Hello, it's me. I'm getting better. Will be back at work in no time, but my mother is in very bad shape." Would he, or could he, give me something to revive her? "Wait a minute," he interrupted, walked into his office and brought out a bottle of red wine. I grabbed it, ran up to mother, put it to her lips, and as she drank it, she opened her eyes, looked at me with a faint smile and said, "Good." That was the turning point. She came through it, recuperated fully, and continued living for a long time. She lived to see and hold her great grandson, with his blue eyes and blonde hair—"The one who came from the Jews." She died clear of mind, in America, in 1984, one year short of a century.

Another unbelievable survival I witnessed was that of Altschul. In his fifties and well aware how slim his chances of survival were, he refused to lie down. He walked around, dragging his stiff leg behind him, his eyes glazed with fever, but would not go to bed. "I'm alright. You all leave me alone." Then, he vanished—for how long, I'm not sure. In those days, we lost our concept of time. We were left alone by the outside world, with few windows, in a mental asylum atmosphere, surrounded by death. Day blended into night and night became day. All were one. Soon we forgot about Altschul's existence.

In a corner of the barn, next to the mill house, was a little shed sometimes used for coal storage, hardly ever approached by anyone. This was the spot in which Altschul chose to fight his battle with typhus—unattended, all by himself. Somehow, he managed to win. One morning, a shaky, dirty black apparition appeared, crawling out of the shed. He was so dirty that, had he remained on top of the heap of coal, he would not have been noticed at all. But perhaps dirt had some healing properties. To everyone's amazement, he became stronger by the day, and within a couple of weeks he was back at work. We finally forced him to take a shower, which was not an easy task. Somehow, cleanliness seemed to cause Altschul great discomfort. I recall that he shaved one evening and left half of the foam on his face until bedtime.

"Altschul," I said, "you can't go to bed this way." His answer: "Oh no? You want to make a bet?" I didn't and he slept like a log.

He also considered himself to be the best chef in the world, always on the lookout for extraordinary delicacies. One night he got hold of some flour and sugar plus a lot of other ingredients, and decided to bake some extraordinary cupcakes. What dish did he use? His own, plus a couple of borrowed shaving cups! He

baked them in my furnace. As if the soap cups were not enough to
spoil our appetites completely, he tested the fluffiness with a
match that had just come out of his ear. What a character! He was
not devoid of a mischievous sense of humor.

With the constant influx of new scapegoats in 1943 came one
named Demeras, who claimed to be a Turk. He insisted vo-
ciferously that he was with us only temporarily and would be
freed as soon as his mistaken identity was clarified. True or false,
for the present he was stuck. He claimed to be an expert auto
mechanic, but personally, I think he was either a slave merchant
or a circus performer. Of medium height and with a neck bigger
than that of a bull, he swung his long whip with a sound and speed
better than any expert I ever met. Many felt its touch on their
backs. This, of course, appealed enormously to Kiski, who put
him in charge of keeping order inside the camp premises.

With lots of time on his hands, he buzzed around all the cars on
the premises, to everyone's annoyance. Lehman inherited him.
When the engine of his vehicle developed a slight whistle, the
Turk assured him that he could fix it within minutes. Well, after a
couple of experiments, the whistle was still there. Lehman, the
Turk, and myself were standing there listening, when in came
Altschul. As usual, his little hammer was in his hand and a foxy
smile on his face. "What's going on?" he asked. Lehman and
Liszek were not Kiski—they never raised a hand nor even abused
anyone verbally. Once in awhile you could even joke with them.
The Turk did not like Altschul, but had no choice and moved
aside. Altschul listened intently, bent over the carburetor, adjusted a couple of screws, and tapped lightly on the outside with
his hammer a couple of times. To the Turk's chagrin, the noise
stopped. Later that evening, Altschul received a nice piece of cake
from Lehman, ate most of it on the spot, walked over to Lehman
again and asked him, with a broad smile, "Could I have another
piece, please?" Lehman looked at him, and half jokingly said, "You
swine, don't you ever have enough? All you did was give it a
couple of knocks with your hammer." "That's true," said Altschul.
"The first piece of cake you gave me was for the couple of knocks.
The other piece I would like for knowing where to knock!"

How our German administrators or whoever managed for
months to keep us out of Auschwitz and total destruction while
typhus worked its devastation will never be explained fully. The

quarantine obviously was effective because despite the proximity, only one German girl (called "the fat Hilda") caught the bug, and she survived. Slowly, the camp started to return to normal. Lehman, in a rush to get us back to work and resume a show of productivity without lifting the quarantine completely, asked Zehngut to select the strongest among us to be sent by truck to dig ditches in a far-out field. The group was picked up every morning by truck. The driver, Franz, whom I befriended quite intimately, was the first German I encountered who was not afraid to express doubts about final victory and openly showed disgust with the way we were treated. His truck was fueled by steam, which was generated by a water boiler mounted in a corner on top of the open truck. Next to it was a pile of cut wood to feed the fire below. By war's end, even passenger cars had boilers attached to the back and trunks full of either pressed wood briquettes or wood pieces. Gasoline was reserved for the army only, with small rations left for party bigshots. This was the way the Germans hoped to ride to final victory. "*Räder müssen rollen für den Sieg*—Wheels must roll towards victory," was the slogan seen everywhere.

Cutting wood for the boiler on top of the truck and lighting the fire before dawn became my early morning routine. By the time Franz arrived, the boiler was hot and ready to go.

Allow me to digress briefly. During all the years in camp, I resorted to producing various items of jewelry. Through the years, I encountered inmates who had been jewelers before the war. I helped them out by getting tools for them and later, let one of them work downstairs in my furnace cubicle. I worked with him, observing and learning about polishing, soldering, and engraving. Unfortunately, this jeweler died during the typhus epidemic. But another friend, a Belgian engraver, survived. While convalescing, I found a lot of time to practice my new profession. I bought a silver spoon for a ration of bread, hammered it flat, and cut six narrow strips, which I bent into ring shanks, then divided them at the ends into a Y-shape which I soldered to a prepared oval or heart-shaped plate. The engraver sold me a couple of inches of paper-thin fourteen-carat gold plate, which I soldered on top of the silver. He engraved the monograms, cutting deep through the gold to get a two-tone effect. Next I filed them into their final shape and polished them, ending up with six smart-looking two-toned silver and gold rings.

Sounds simple? Wait until I describe my soldering and polishing equipment! The polishing machine consisted of part of a long strip of rag saturated with rouge-polish compound. One end of it I held with my teeth; the other end with my left hand. With my right hand I moved the ring up and down vigorously, until after a while I would achieve a decent shine. Soldering was done the ancient Egyptian way, holding a thin tube in my mouth through which I blew oxygen to increase the intensity of the flame produced by my tiny wood-alcohol lamp. This operation gave me a great deal of trouble after my jeweler friend died. It could only be mastered with years of training and I melted and ruined quite a few almost-finished items.

Worst of all, however, were the thin sawblades. Any jeweler will understand and sympathize with my plight. A professional, working in a rush, will easily break a dozen blades in an hour. I had moments when I was down to my last one and knew it might be weeks, if ever, before I could get a replacement, because during the war they were extremely hard to get. I simply could not afford to break one; I used most blades until there were no more teeth left, but I rarely broke one. One of my rings could easily buy a loaf of bread. I had to make two and sometimes three rings to get half a dozen blades. I had nightmares over those blades. As you may have guessed by now, this remained my profession in later life, and through the years I have always made sure to have at least a hundred gross on hand so that I could break them like mad and feel safe.

But let us return to the quarantine, my friend Franz, and his truck. I correctly judged him to be a fellow who would enjoy taking risks. I produced a number of rings for him and a name pin for his girlfriend. He smiled when I told him what I had in mind. We had been quarantined now for more than two months without any contact with the girls who had left for Peterswaldau. I knew they must be going out of their minds worrying about what had happened to us in the hellhole of Gräditz, wondering who was alive and who was not. Personally, I took the risk only because of Dorka, knowing she worried about her brother and me. I prepared a letter containing the sad list of the unfortunate victims who were next-of-kin of the twenty girls.

Usually the driver sat at the wheel by himself, the one guard who accompanied us up on the truck watching the inmates. Under his seat, Franz had a large storage space for parts and tools. He emptied it a day before we were to carry out our plan, and let me crawl in there and hide. We had surveyed and carefully timed the route beforehand so that we knew exactly when the girls would be crossing the little, narrow bridge every day on their way to work. When we reached the bridge that morning, his engine, as planned, stopped. He jumped out and opened the hood, making believe he was busy fixing it. At the same time he yelled up to the guard to keep a careful eye on the prisoners, who were still supposed to be quarantined, and not let them mingle with the outside world. When the girls began to cross the bridge, he started the engine. This was my signal. I slid out of the bow and stuck my shaven head through the window. Rita, Berek's future wife, saw my bald skull and shrunken pale face coming through the window. From her bewildered appearance, I knew she was not sure whether it was really me. (An hour later Franz's girlfriend, who worked nearby, delivered my list. Only then were they convinced that it was me.) I slid back into my box, Franz jumped back into the truck and we drove on to deliver the brigade to their workstation.

When we got back, half of the convalescing camp was still asleep. I walked into Zehngut's room and told him, "Sir, I have regards for you from Peterswaldau." Still half asleep, he looked at me, thinking that I was hallucinating from my bout with typhus, and told me to get out of the room and let him sleep. Much later that day he found me and listened to what I had to say. He got mad and screamed at me, but could not hide the smile on his face.

Slowly, the survivors began to regain their strength. Many had strange and frequent lapses of reason, telling funny, idiotic stories in the middle of a perfectly normal conversation. It was frightening at first, until we realized that this was a passing stage; then we joked about it and called them "calkheads," a reference to calcium in the brain. Step by step, we started back to work. One of the first groups was employed at Diehl's ammunition factory, working in close proximity to the girls, so that we could engage in a fairly regular correspondence. As a precaution, we used pseudonyms and Dorka became "Zosia" (Sofie).

There were two kinds of romances in the camps: the affairs *du coeur* and the affairs of the stomach.

The stomach affairs lasted only as long as the dire need of food

existed, leaving many girls bewildered and heartbroken the minute food became available. Conversely, the genuine attachments
became permanent and were enormously helpful in easing our
struggles. The resolve to survive gained power; we wrote to each
other white lies about the imminent end of the war or painted
rosy pictures of tomorrow. And it helped. The trouble was that
the yearning and waiting dragged on endlessly and our imagina-
tions eventually ran dry. Then our moods would darken deeply
once again.

Gräditz went back to work full-swing. The survivors, drained
and sad in their squalid quarters, tried to adjust to life after
typhus as well as they could. Lehman and Liszek, his right-hand
man, left the daily headaches to Zehngut and his helpers, partying
and living it up like creatures who knew that their good times
were coming to an end.

Once in the middle of the night, I felt someone pulling my
sleeve. I opened one eye and who did I see but Mr. Lehman
himself. Half tipsy, he whispered, "Techniker, Techniker, get up.
Get up! Come with me." I slipped on my trousers and shoes and
followed him. Swaying down the steps from the left to right, he
led me to the kitchen.

Matchky, the cook, locked the door of the storage room every
night behind him. (He knew with whom he was dealing.) In the
upper half of that locked door was a little sliding window opening
through which to pass items called for in the process of cooking.
Lehman lifted me up halfway and helped to push me through
that little opening—a tight squeeze, but I made it. Once inside, he
asked me to pass out several bottles of wine, *Kuchen* (cake), plus an
assortment of goodies. Then he dragged me back outside, put a
finger on his lips and said, "Silence, Techniker . . . silence.
Gute Nacht."

The orgy across the yard went on all night. We knew it because
we had to clean up the awful mess next morning.

It was either late fall 1943 or the spring of 1944. The Germans
somehow found themselves with nine hundred Ukrainian soldiers, convalescing from typhus, with no place to go. They were
soldiers of the infamous Ukrainian traitor Andrei Vlasov. At their
wit's end, the Germans finally decided to stick them into the old
flour mill house of Gräditz, together with the leftover Jews who
were inflicted with the same disease. And so we were all crammed

into the same cage—beast and man alike! Strange as it may seem, Jews and Ukrainians found they shared one thing in common: they both died for Hitler.

Out of embarrassment, the Germans attempted to build walls to divide us, but this was a pure exercise in futility. Half dead and disgusted, we all managed to live together in peace for a while. Because we shared the heat and water supply, I had a constant and undisturbed contact with them. One Sunday afternoon, their leader called on me in the furnace room, upset about a problem he had. The German authorities had made available to them three boxes of cigarettes, fifty each, two loaves of bread, a bottle of wine, and two boxes of shoe polish, all at the ridiculously low price of 16 marks and 85 pennies. His problem was there was no way in the world he could come up with the money. Could I perhaps think of something? Well, I could hardly contain my excitement. I asked him to give me some time and I would see what I could do. That was too big a deal to handle by myself. A hundred and fifty thousand D. marks, a hundred and thirty-five thousand ciga-rettes, wine and bread on top of it—an unimaginable fortune in a place where inmates were ready to fight and kill over a cigarette butt! I have seen people, hardly able to walk, trade half of their tiny bread ration for three cigarettes. Do we know anything about the power of addiction?

For a short moment, I suspected a trap, but just as quickly disregarded the notion as nonsense. This was a simple case of inadequacy, vividly underlining our differences: our ability to take advantage of any opportunity as opposed to their inability to do so despite their overwhelmingly favorable conditions. Within a few days, with the help of the always resourceful Mannes Schwarz, I had the money in hand and a team ready to distribute the cigarettes, part to the girls' camp and part among ourselves. The deal I offered to the Ukrainians was simple: they would get all the money they needed; I would take one hundred cigarettes plus one loaf of bread. They accepted with delight, thus obtaining bread and wine, cigarettes, and shoe polish at no cost. The phys-ical transfer was not simple, but having relative freedom of inter-nal movement because the guards were still fearful of the disease, we somehow managed.

That deal could not have come at a better time. Eventually, the Ukrainians took over Gräditz completely, and we were transferred into the genuine, full-fledged concentration camp, *Sports-chule*, a division of the terrible *Grossrosen* concentration camp. Those cigarettes fed our family and friends for months to come, as we found ourselves once more in a new, strange, and gruesome environment.

8
"Sportschule"—1944

The second half of 1944 found us in that grim place, located near Reichenbach. After years of incarceration, typhus, emaciation, our bodies and hopes depleted beyond believable limits of human endurance, one more ordeal was in store for us. Having to give up our own clothes in exchange for a gray-blue striped burlap uniform dealt a powerful blow to our spirits. We were now vividly marked, beyond any possible doubt. They took the final precautionary step of cutting our hair, or rather tearing it off with a dull hand-operated barber machine, to a length of about half an inch. A perfect porcupine look—not bad; but we were not finished yet. Finally, they cut through the middle, front to back, a dull one-and-a-half-inch wide, very short, clipped strip. We looked pathetic. I was glad that there were no mirrors around. While daydreaming during those years, I had often imagined the moment of the war's end: pandemonium reigning all around, the prisoners escaping from their pursuers and mingling for safety with the civilian population. But no more! Now, we were sitting ducks—marked until our hair grew in, or we shaved our heads, or changed our clothes . . . and for that, one needed time, in a situation where seconds can mean life or death.

Having no other choices, we had once more to accept and adapt to our new, depressing gray landscape and pathetic appearance.

Eventually most of us were employed in Diehl's ammunition factory. There, in addition to other benefits, I had a chance to see and sometimes even exchange a few words with Dorka. For her, this was not always a blessing. Each time she was caught speaking to me she was beaten and threatened with a head shave by her blond female guard. But just as fear didn't stop Romeo and Juliet, so it did not stop us from using every opportunity to exchange a few words.

The other benefit of working at Diehl's was the availability of aluminum sheets, heating spirals, and insulating material. We worked around the clock in three shifts, because the army needed the trigger timing devices we manufactured very badly. The night shifts were torturous nightmares. The boredom of mass production made fighting sleep impossible, resulting in many injuries. On rare occasions during those long nights, we got a little relief— suddenly, darkness, a power failure; foremen running around looking for the cause. In would come Altschul, his mischievous smile on his face, calling me over and whispering in my ear. "Go take a snooze for at least a couple of hours; they'll never find it before then." He was right, and we would have a beautiful two-hour rest. Those little pranks, bringing us so close to disaster, broke the terrible monotony and helped us to persevere.

Being employed in the maintenance and repair section, I had enough freedom and opportunity to make use of the raw material available to produce the ever-in-demand containers and heating plates. My great coup, as I mentioned before, was the *menashka* I made for the all-powerful *Judenaltester* B. Meister. That gift granted me a few weeks of repair work in the all-girl camp of Peterswaldau. Ironically, Dorka was always away working at the Diehl factory.

When we left Gräditz, we did not take any women with us. Mother wound up working at another ammo factory in Langenbielau, and because all those places were within a three-mile radius I often found opportunities to send her some food.

One evening after work, Berek and I were sitting on the lower bunk, spooning our soup ration out of one dish, saving the other for later on or possibly the next day. Berek's behavior seemed strange. He was eating like a wild man—he could not control his hunger. I became alarmed. This was our fourth year of sharing food without any incidents or problems, a practice that was one of the great pillars of our strength. We had witnessed brothers dividing their rations with the help of a homemade little scale, which shocked us at first. Later on we had seen much worse—fights over food between relatives and even fathers and sons. What was most surprising was that the most extreme examples seemed to come from people one used to look up to before the war, envying their well-being and stature in our community, whereas a lot of quiet simpletons behaved with unexpected nobility. Between Berek and myself, even a scale would have been unthinkable, so I knew immediately that something must have gone wrong. And it had. Berek happened to be working near my mother's camp, so I had entrusted him with a loaf of bread to deliver to her. Unfortunately, someone had stolen it from him. Those happened to be very lean days, and Berek tried to make up the loss by cutting in half his daily ration. It nearly killed him; luckily for both of us, he forgot himself and started eating abnormally.

Having no previous military training or weapons, we were in no position to fight our enemies. The only defenses left were our wits and our unbroken spirit. At this juncture, our spirits were reaching the limits, which makes Berek's deed even more remarkable.

Standing on the dirty bare soil of the camp were about eight rectangular three-story gray blocks where we lived. We had only cold water, and drums to urinate in during the night. A bunch of emaciated striped ghosts, constantly dragging along through the dark corridors, it's small wonder that our moods reached the lowest of ebbs. Yet despite the debilitating effects of our squalid surroundings, at the least likely time, and under the worst conditions, I turned again to making jewelry. In the evening after gulping down my chow, I would stick a board between two beds, and with one of my buddies always on the lookout to warn me in time to hide my meager but precious equipment, I went to work, ironically, producing the luxuries of life. I could not wait to get back to the plant each morning, where I had the luxury of mechanically polishing and finishing my products, all under the watchful eyes of my German foremen, who also happened to be my customers. It was a dual blessing: besides earning extra food, I found that time passed very quickly.

The Beginning of the End

The war dragged on endlessly. We lost interest in news. The victories of the Allies that we heard about stopped impressing us, because they were not meant for us anymore. We became increasingly fatalistic as we realized that the Germans were determined to win at any cost. What chance was there for us? Roosevelt was reelected; the Germans laughed. They circulated crude and depressing jokes: All the new toilet bowls in America will have Roosevelt's picture, so the assholes can see who they voted for!

They laughed and we cried. The prospect of another winter was not something to look forward to.

I ran out of the positive interpretations of current events that I usually composed for my letters to Dorka. The great optimism was waning rapidly.

And then! One cloudy day, they came. We could not see them; we could only hear the hum of that heavenly armada passing over us on the way to bomb some more important targets, their cargo pregnant with death mixed with hope of life. They passed all too quickly. We had to go back and continue our silly, futile chores. We were wrapping precision machinery hermetically in plastic sheets, to be submerged in a nearby lake. The Germans planned to retrieve the machinery right after the counteroffensive had pushed the Russians back.

The bombers were gone! Deeply disappointed and depressed, we silently prayed: Come on! Come back! Rain some terror from the sky! . . . *"Let me die with the Philistines"* (Samson).

As the days passed we could not, despite our pessimism, ignore the obvious signs of change. We continued marching daily to work under the same rigor, perhaps even more severe now on account of the military defeats and bombings of German cities. Few of our tormentors mellowed; most became more adamant. We had to keep our mouths shut and our eyes lowered. Inside our camp, we got a twenty-year-old Wehrmacht animal who beat everyone in sight, indiscriminately. We named him, appropriately, "The Animal." He tried to deal a blow for every bomb that hit Germany. His superiors, who were more mature and wiser, could not contain him. When the Russians got closer, he vanished. Too bad!

Rumors were flying. The most feared possibility was evacuation. In the history of the Holocaust, those evacuations near the end of the war are a close second to the gas chambers. Some of the inmates, emaciated after years of hunger and torture, were put on open freight trains going west; most marched westward. Those who did not die on the train were shot along the roadside when they could walk no longer. Some, like myself, spent close to four years waiting for the great day. Finally they saw the light approaching, only to be cut down before they reached the Promised Land. Their memory evokes in me the deepest frustrations and doubts about the existence of justice. My favorite poet said it so well:

You always rule. You always ridicule.
Liars are those who call you love—All you are is thought.
You look upon a million souls pleading for salvation as merely
An intricate book balancing equation!

                   —Adam Mickiewicz

Another episode from those days drives my point home clearly. On Yom Kippur most of us fasted, even those who had never done so at home. Under the circumstances it was easy and gave us a feeling of victorious defiance. One of our group was a rabbi. In an outburst of overwhelming frustration he threw his shovel away, turned his eyes toward heaven, and cried out, "Almighty! Would you forget us for awhile and leave us alone! We had enough being your Chosen Ones—Let us try without your help!" Exhausted, he picked up his shovel and resumed digging.

All during the spring of 1945 rumors of the dreaded evacuation persisted. It is conceivable that the infamous *Judenältester* B Meister redeemed himself in those crucial hours. If it is true that the final decision to evacuate was in the hands of our local S.S. *Lagerkommandant,* then it was Meister, who had a great influence over him, who kept convincing him to postpone the march from day to day, until it was too late. Watching him, in the last hours, removing the S.S. epaulets and insignias designating his rank, corroborated my supposition.

9

Liberation

Those last days were filled with a mixture of hope and apprehension. We feared that the final convulsions of the monster in whose grasp we still were would somehow manage to destroy us before we would see the first Russian soldier. Finally, the month of May crept in, and on the eighth day, the Germans watching over us disappeared. We opened the gates and fearfully ventured out. The numbness of those first moments produced a semi-amnesia. I can only recall it through a haze. After reuniting with Mother and Dorka, we took up residence in one of the abandoned houses in Reichenbach. Striped uniforms hung from the trees of the town for days. The inmates, dressed in whatever they could find, were already changed beyond recognition. Bernard and I went "hunting" for some fitting clothes, and came back on two bicycles. Dorka laughed, looked at her brother, and asked him where he had left me behind. He smiled. Then she looked a second time at the fellow next to him in a leather outfit and finally recognized me. Who remembered or thought of revenge? The euphoria was so overwhelming that all serious thoughts vanished. Reality stopped existing for awhile; revenge could wait. For the moment we were satisfied to wipe our feet on an entrance mat made of a Wehrmacht colonel's uniform. By the time we realized the extent of their murderous accomplishments, it was too late. Law and order was re-established and Germans were humanely treated and protected. No one was guilty; the innocent citizenry objected to being forced to look at the atrocities many of them had personally performed. By now, the uniforms and records were well hidden.

For the first few days, hardly any Russians were to be seen. Hunger had not reached the point in our camp that it did in Belzen and other death camps, where a bit of overindulgence killed so many after liberation. So we went on an eating spree to our tummies' delight. The Red Army was in control of food; the German butchers and bakers who had not run away were kept busy day and night. The individual Russian soldiers liked to oblige by supplying poultry, having fun chasing after the chickens. In the beginning, we had fun with them, but then they started looking for rewards—and money was not on their minds. Thus the first signs of crude reality reappeared. Some incidents were serious, especially those involving girls without their own male companions. One girl was shot resisting rape five days after liberation. Many of the soldiers were uncontrollable; the term "concentration camp" had no meaning for them. In the midst of all the euphoria, ugly incidents were taking place with increasing frequency.

After about a week of living in limbo, thoughts of "What now?" started edging into our consciousness. A number of boys ran futilely to Poland in search of family. The only transportation available was hitchhiking on Russian army trucks—a dangerous undertaking, to say the least. We decided to stay in place for the time being and wait to see what would develop. Contrary to our great expectations, no one came to greet us or shower us with gifts or apologies for not being able to help us sooner. We made a few halfhearted attempts to catch up with some of the most notorious guards, but they were all gone. After all, they were on their own soil, without a visible sign of Cain on their foreheads. The Russians made themselves at home in Reichenbach and did not especially like our proximity. The German female population did not offer nearly as much resistance as did the Jewish girls. The soldiers felt that their comrades did not get killed simply to rehabilitate Hitler's Jewish scapegoats, and they wanted the full spoils of victory. All rewards are reserved for those who stay alive. Reichenbach was a nice, clean little German town, so the Red Army military command decided to make it *Judenrein* once again. To our unbelievable dismay they asked us to pack, gave us a couple of soldiers for company, and sent us on our way to the next big city. How quickly history repeats itself! Shocked, outraged, but with no one to complain to, we set out on our way.

Epilogue

My story would not be complete without an account of the happenings of the next few months.

Breslau

Anything that happened to us after liberation was delightful, even the disappointments. We were no longer primarily Jews; every other kind of abuse was easy to cope with. After leaving Reichenbach, we walked about 60 kilometers to Breslau. I don't remember how long it took. On the road, we encountered Russian soldiers minesweeping the fields. A strange group loaded with packages, we attracted their attention. We tried to tell them that they had liberated us from Hitler's concentration camps. They looked puzzled; I tried to explain in Polish. I said to them, "Hitler. Hitler," and motioned cutting my neck. Ah, one started smiling. "Gitler, Gitler, oh, da, da." What interested them more was the *Charosza Dziewószka, Krasnaya,* beautiful, pretty girl. Well, that was the end of our friendly conversations; quickly we continued on our road.

We arrived in Breslau at a municipal building of some sort. The two soldiers who accompanied us vanished inside, and we stood around for a long time, not knowing what to do next. Along came a strange-looking civilian sporting a moustache of the size mustered by the ancient Polish Hussars. He addressed us in Polish, inquiring what we were doing here. After listening to our agitated account of the last couple of days, he shook his head, smiling, and told us, "Forget the soldiers; you are now in Breslau. The city is under Polish command. Go find an empty apartment, of which there are plenty. Make yourselves comfortable and come to see me whenever you are ready. I will see what I can do about some kind of employment. We are desperate for capable people who are willing to work. My name is Dr. Wilk and I am the judge in charge of the civil court. Do not worry. You are free now. Call on me if you need help."

It sounded too good to be true, but true it was. We spent the next few months in the city of Breslau, where I got a job through Dr. Wilk in the vehicle depot of the Polish Army under the auspices of the Division of Security. Ignorant of the ways of the world, surrounded by hundreds of broken cars in need of repair, it did not dawn on me that I was working for the Polish KGB. I was assigned to the garage; Berek was assigned to a desk job interrogating Germans suspected of evil doing. We wondered where this would bring us, but decided to sit back a while and observe. We discovered many Jewish boys in Polish uniforms, full of smiles, enjoying their status of conquerors. They had lived through the war in Russia, and being Polish citizens, they were assigned to duty with a Polish division, which, in turn, was totally under Russian control.

Knowing that all of this was temporary and not knowing that to do or where to go, we just let the dice roll and enjoyed our newfound freedom. I was offered a rank and a uniform, which I refused, but I accepted a motorcycle and rode to work like a king. Sometimes I took my neighbor, a Russian captain, along with me to his headquarters, on the back seat of my motorcycle. I was in charge of six top-notch auto mechanics, the very best Breslau had to offer. Our primary task was to remove the silly water boilers attached to all passenger cars, restoring them to their original form for the use of gasoline. Breslau had a huge cemetery of old vehicles that would be the envy of any large city. A capable car bug could, with patience, put together almost any vehicle of his choice without a trip to a supply house. And in June of 1945, this was the only supply house in existence.

I learned more about cars in those two months than I did in all my previous years. Among many interesting things, we dug up a buried Mercedes that had been specially built for the infamous Governor Frank, the butcher of Poland. Outfitted with a sixteen-cylinder V engine, it was custom built for two passengers, plus a seat for an armed guard in the back. Red upholstery was edge-lined with silver. One morning, I asked one of the soldiers with a machine gun to come along, and with a chauffeur we drove home. I honked the horn. Dorka and the family stepped out on the balcony to gaze below at that enormously long stretch of beauty.

But the fun was short-lived; we had to hide it by burying it quickly again, because the Russians were ready to grab it for themselves. Their favorite sport was to raid our garage in the middle of the night, seizing the best and nicest vehicles that we had sweated for days to put together. Because we could not reach Stalin to complain, we learned quickly not to display anything valuable.

The person in charge of the establishment I worked in was a Polish guy who was primarily interested in two things: fishing and drinking. I came in very handy; now, instead of indulging his interests only in the evening, he could pursue them all day, especially fishing. He was not what one would call a noble angler, a true sportsman. I would define him more appropriately as a killer of fish. The method he used was to fill a tightly corked glass bottle with quick (raw) lime, shake it vigorously, and throw it into the lake. The ensuing explosion would burst the membrane of the poor fish, which then floated to the top—an easy catch. One day, he made a fatal mistake: he held the bottle in his hand for a moment too long. And that's how I became the chief of operations, responsible for supplying vehicles for the Russian-controlled Polish army in Breslau.

Everything in life is relative. Next to the Germans, the Russians were great. Nevertheless, it was not easy to like them. For example, Bernard rode a bicycle to work. One day a Russian soldier saw it, liked it, put the gun to his head, took the bike, and away he rode, leaving Bernard with his mouth wide open. My neighbor, the captain who claimed to be Jewish, watched me cleaning my motorcycle one afternoon. I took off one of the wheels. He looked it over, picked it up, and said to me, "I will take it to my room. When you're ready to put it back, come on up." I found this rather strange, but complied. Half an hour later, I went to claim it. I found him sitting comfortably on a chair, his revolver displayed ostentatiously on top of the table, next to my wheel. I looked first at the revolver, then at the wheel, then at him, with a question mark on my face. He began by telling me that he is about to send a package home and wants to send along my wheel and, by the way, he said, what will my boy do with a motorcycle with only one wheel? Why not give him the rest of it so he can send the whole thing to his family back home? Without the experience of World War II behind me, I probably would have done something foolish. I might even have succeeded in holding onto my possession. But in June 1945, I was not about to jeopardize my life on account of a motorcycle. Angry, I blurted out the Hebrew word, "Shalom," and walked out. This was an experience no less shocking than many of the past six years.

By this time I was convinced that our move from Reichenbach had been in the wrong direction. While continuing in my capacity at the garage, I kept one eye always concentrated on the exit. Shortly thereafter, I had a minor disagreement with my immediate superior, a party bigshot. We settled the dispute and before I left his office I expressed the wish to be released in the near future to further my education. He looked at me angrily; I suspect he was a little tipsy. Then he blurted out, "We do not release anyone here. The only release you can get is against the wall!" This was more than I was prepared to take from anyone. I would be embarrassed to repeat the foul language I used in reply. Within a few days, on August 30, 1945, I took one of the cars and drove to the headquarters in Lignice and confronted the famous partisan fighter, Major Yemiolka, who was the man in charge of the whole security operation. He listened to me, cursed, and turned me over to the Secretary of the Communist Party, Ms. Opalko. She tried to calm me, offering a prestigious position in any town of my choice in Poland. I replied that while I appreciated her trust in my abilities, I did not endure Hitler all those years to become a city official, no matter how lucrative the position. "Thank you," I said, "but my education was interrupted and my first duty is to continue it for the benefit of everyone involved, including the new free Poland." Against this argument, she had no recourse and reluctantly gave me an honorable discharge. The document is still in my possession.

During my days of service at the car depot, we had befriended Mr. T., the man in charge of the Polish Security Unit of Breslau. After my discharge, I got to see him quite often. Dr. Wilk was also one of the frequent visitors in his house. Being top brass, he occupied a very spacious apartment, located within walking distance from our own. We all realized by then that it did not make much sense to remain under existing circumstances in the east, and clandestinely we were all preparing to make it to the British or American zones of the occupation. It was impossible for all members of the family to travel at once. Dorka, her brother, mother, some six cousins, Berek and some friends—in total we were a family of more than twelve. So we decided to split up. Barnard with one cousin succeeded in getting over to Munich first; then Dorka and a couple more followed. Mother and I were supposed to try a couple of days later. We all had to cross a Russian border to get into the American or British zones. Armed with all kinds of documents and excuses—such as that we were searching for lost family members—with a little fear and much trepidation, the exodus was underway.

Unknown to me, Mr. T. decided to abscond at the same time. He was a high official deserting his post, a very serious matter, to put it mildly. During the last month we were in the habit of dropping into his house for a chat and an aperitif. I walked over alone this particular evening. His wife greeted me and I mentioned to her that Dorka couldn't make it today and I would stay only a couple of minutes. We stood around reminiscing and politicking a while and when I got ready to leave, two men in trench coats (they were almost a permanent fixture in this house) stopped me, saying, "No one can leave the house as yet."

At this point I realized that I had not seen the host, so naturally, I asked to see the master of the house. "Sorry," they said. "He is not available. Would you please sit down and make yourself comfortable." This was strange and seemed very suspicious. A half hour passed, and one of Dorka's three cousins came to see why I had let them wait with the dinner. She got stuck. Within a half an hour, her sister came to inquire what had happened, and she got stuck; then the third sister and my mother came along. Within two hours, close to one hundred people were gathered in that strange apartment that let people come in but let nobody go out.

By nine o'clock, a couple of police station wagons arrived, and took the whole bunch down to headquarters for interrogation. Mother and a few more elderly people were released and sent home. For the rest of us, it was into the slammer, where I spent the next two weeks. The sequence of steps that I described was a routine method used to exhaust all possibility of getting an accidental clue. It must have worked in many cases, but it did not accomplish anything that evening. Most of the group were released after a couple of days, but they kept T.'s brother, his wife, a couple of close friends, and me for two weeks. I suspected all the time that they were holding me because of my previous employment, but I found out later that they did not even make the connection. By then, I was learning not to look for logical explanations where the Russians' actions were concerned.

Dorka, in the meantime, was on the road with many others, trying to get through to the British or American zones. One of them, coincidentally, was none other than Mr. T. He was not easily recognized without his uniform. In later years, to Dorka's chagrin, he teased her that while Shlamek was in jail with his wife, T. was Dorka's constant companion!

After a number of mishaps and nerve-wracking border crossings, we were all finally united in Munich, Germany, in the American zone. Sleeping ten in one little room, we were constantly receiving additional tenants. But this did not diminish in the least our ecstasy at leaving the Russians and Poles behind us.

So ends my story of that dark period. After four years of concentration camps, plus a taste of the Russians; after surviving hundreds of reckless risks, but fortunately never having to face making the ultimate choice or standing in front of the barrel of a gun; alive with my family, and still sane according to the standards of our society, what more can I say than, Thank you, my lucky star.

Plato's dream of utopia has eluded us for more than two thousand years and will probably continue to do so. Kings will not be philosophers; philosophers will never be kings. Until human beings learn to control greed and accept the limitations of their powers, there will be more persecutions, wars, and Holocausts. So let's keep our eyes open and beware.

"Jacob's Face"

"When Joseph was confronted with the ultimate temptation his father's face appeared."
—Rashi (chap. 49, v. 26, quoting the *Talmud*)

Do we have the right to expect the world to remember? Can Jews in general and survivors in particular have a moral justification for feeling comfortable in and enjoying a car manufactured by Mercedes Benz or BMW (Bayrische Motoren Werke), the two companies who so unreservedly contributed to Hitler's successes? The justification one commonly hears is more galling than the act itself. Israel does it. How can anyone compare a painful reciprocal agreement between two countries (one filthy rich, trying to atone for its crimes, the other one gasping for breath) to a personal choice of a luxury item . . . a choice made while numerous options are readily available. The sting is felt most painfully in synagogue parking lots.

I must confess that once I walked into a Mercedes showroom myself. The unmistakably Jewish salesman with an unmistakably German obsequious smile (or was it my imagination?) approached me with his sales pitch for the well-made car whose image, through the power of advertising and clever merchandising, has become synonymous with excellence. I could not refuse the invitation to enter. I slid easily into the luxurious leather upholstery and was immediately overwhelmed by the excellent quality of sound from the speakers. The music? Von Karajan conducting Wagner . . . Irresistible? Then luckily I made the mistake of opening the easy sliding ashtray.

I found it full of ashes.

And the wall came tumbling down
And the guilt and dirt got buried underneath
With us gone, who will ever dig it up? . . . . S.G.

"Great Performances"

In pre-Hitler Vienna, Mr. Volf (Herr Wolf) was a famous, much-in-demand night club star. His knowledge of, or contact with, Judaism was probably about equal to that of an Eskimo in far away Lapland.

In the spring of 1944 he was recuperating from typhus in Gräditz. With the little life left in him he tried to entertain us fellow inmates, hoping to get an extra bowl of soup. With his demented puffed up face, bags under his eyes down to his jaw, his color the unmistakable pale purple of death, his limbs swollen beyond belief, he stood there belting out his song. *"Sonne liebe Sonne"*: Sun—dear—sun—won't you come, and visit me once again? Won't you let your life giving rays touch me once more? I am so frozen and need you so badly!" Once a showman always a showman!

His voice betraying his utter resignation, he gave a most sincere and touching performance. In all my life I never witnessed a greater one.

Where were you hiding, Splendid Silent Sun?